UPPER BUNKIES UNITE

AND OTHER THOUGHTS ON THE POLITICS OF MASS INCARCERATION

By

Andrea C. James

With a Foreword by James P. Comer, M.D.

GOODE BOOK PRESS
www.goodebookpress.com

Goode Book Press
PO Box 248
Boston, MA 02121

All Goode Book Press titles are available at special quantity discounts for bulk purchases for sale promotion, premiums, fund-raising, educational or institutional use.

Special book excerpts or customized printings can also be created to fit specific needs. For details, write or phone the office of the Goode Book Press sales office: Goode Book Press, PO Box 248, Boston, MA 02121. Phone: (617) 905-2026

Goode Book Press and the Goode Book Press logo Reg. U.S. Pat. & TM Off.

Library of Congress Control Number: 2013932809

First Printing March 2013

Cover design by Tone Spin Designs
Edited by Dolores E. Goode, Ph.D

Printed in the United States of America

Andrea C. James

UPPER BUNKIES UNITE

AND OTHER THOUGHTS ON THE POLITICS OF MASS INCARCERATION

Andrea James is also the author of A *Letter To My Children from A Mad, Black, Incarcerated Mother,* and *My Grandparents Are Polar Bears,* a children's book. She is the co-founder of the advocacy organization, Families for Justice as Healing, www.justiceashealing.org, and the creator of Career Roadmap for Girls, www.careerroadmapforgirls.com. Andrea lives in Massachusetts with her husband, Jon James, and their children.

For my cousin, Paul

ACKNOWLEDGMENTS

I know two things for sure. Writing this book saved my life and gave me a purpose at a time when I didn't know how to pick up the pieces and, I couldn't have written this book or withstood my time in prison without the love and support of the following people.

My prison family, especially Monique Williams and all the women that got me through every moment in that place!

My dear friends Catherine Hoffman and Betty Burkes. With the help of Phillip Bailey and all the books you kept us supplied with, you did more than support me. You helped start a movement.

To my sisterfriend circle, Angelita Green, Kass Thomas-Corbelli and Detria Wisdom, thank you for being mothers to my children. Thank you for the energy that you continued sending to me the entire time and for all the pictures I lined my locker with to remind me of who I was and where I belonged. And thank you for the visits. To Auntie Darla, thank you for your unconditional love and the reminders to simply sit.

To my parents, thank you for the life and education you provided me. Thank you for continuing to help raise the children and thank you for coming to my defense. I love you.

To my children, you stood tall and firm. Never waivered and stayed on course. I love you.

To my husband. You held us all together. I received a visit every single weekend from you. Six hours round trip and you always showed up. May we continue to always show up for each other. I love you. I thank God for you and all of our blessings.

CONTENTS

FOREWORD

James P. Comer, M.D., M.P.H

This is a very important book. The heartfelt story told here, with skill and compassion, is one of our nation's dirty little secrets. And I am afraid we will try to run away from it even here. But we should not. It is too costly in both financial and human terms. Indeed, It is the hole in our "democracy bucket" that can bring us down despite the remarkable journey of progress we have made as a nation. The situation is all the more frustrating and sad when we know that the "cradle to prison pipeline" problem that we are confronted with need not exist; that most of the people caught in the line could be contributing positively toward creating the great society that we want.

As I read the stories of the women who are not much different, if at all, than you and I and the author, Andrea James, herself a former trial lawyer who served 18 months in prison, I was reminded of the comments of my mother, Maggie, who said, "They put me on the garbage heap of life but they could not keep me there." In Maggie's American Dream I helped her tell her oral history; how she got off the garbage heap—an abused child from extreme poverty in rural Mississippi who attended school less than two years because her cruel stepfather did not believe in education; ran away to East Chicago, Indiana; worked as a domestic; found my father, a steel mill worker with about six years of education; and through lives rooted in a positive church culture; they provided me and my four siblings with a developmental experience that enabled us to obtain 13 college degrees. But as importantly, that experience encouraged us to care about people who were less fortunate.

While I was doing my medical internship in my hometown preparing to become a general practitioner there, I noted my three childhood friends were on a downhill life course; one spent a good part of his life in jail. Only the quality of family care and style was different. There were similar levels of parental education, jobs, and income. There was similar intelligence and attendance in the same racially integrated schools. What happened? Why? Seeking answers to these fundamental questions on how to promote better outcomes for similar young people put me on a professional career journey through public health, psychiatry, child and adolescent development, and into schools that we used as prevention sites.

It was our family life that gave us the capacity to make an emotional attachment to school people and to elicit a positive, supportive response from them; to sense belonging, worth and value at home and at school. This provided us with the competencies and confidence to do well academically and socially, leading to even more positive feedback and an upward spiral. My friends, through no fault of their own or their parents, were not prepared to elicit a positive response; often elicited negative responses.

For example, in a contest designed to help us learn to use the library, I read and reported on the most books and won. My three friends did not read a single book. Our teacher, with much irritation, said, “If you three little colored boys don’t want to be like the rest of us you should not come to OUR school.” They did not feel or know that belonging was a major part of the reason they had not participated in the first place. While a culture of racism was at play, this was as much a reflection of poor preparation of educators. All of this was encumbered by a deep-seated tendency in our society to reject, demean, and punish unacceptable performance, regardless of the causes, rather than embrace, include, teach and encourage appropriate and high level performance.

My "colored" status was not mentioned. In fact, it had to be ignored. Poor performance and/or inferiority had to be used to justify the enslavement, exploitation and abuse of a people in an almost theocratic, democratic society committed to liberty and justice for all. These notions of inferiority had to be found and noted repeatedly to remain valid. They became a part of our nation's collective unconscious with multiple carriers from the schoolhouse to the jailhouse. And in the real world pecking order some of the most vigorous "inferiority" belief enforcers are not much better off from an economic, social and psychological standpoint than the people they demean.

My journey for understanding, prevention and the promotion of better opportunities and outcomes for able young people who did not receive the critical ingredient that I received—a good developmental experience at home and then in school—led me to higher education. The focus for change had to be the schools because the industrial job that eventually took my father's life but allowed him to adequately provide for his family without a high level education was disappearing forever and for all. But it could not be the education enterprise that failed to adequately prepare my teacher because in turn, that adversely affected my friends and confused and challenged my own identity and confidence.

I argued that school could provide a supportive community. I maintained that community support could promote parent or caretaker and educator collaboration. Such inclusion would foster a sense of belonging and adequacy in a way that could promote student development, improve academic learning and reinforce the foundation for successful adult life regardless of the present and future complexity of the economy or social system. My vision was that of the school as a caring community.

Our Yale Child Study Center School Development Program (SDP), working in the two lowest achievement elementary schools in New Haven, Connecticut, beginning in 1968, achieved such outcomes. These schools rose from the lowest two in achievement to near the top in a city of 33 schools with best attendance, and no serious behavior problems—in but a few years, at a modest cost. Proud but curious about the acclaim the work was receiving my mother asked me what we did. I described a school curriculum and activities that pretty much provided the students with what she and my dad had provided us. She looked at me in dismay and said, "But that's common sense!" She paused, and then said, "And they pay you for that!"

The approach is common sense based on good judgment and sensible behavior, and in my parent's case, native intelligence. Our SDP applied specialized knowledge from research, training and practice and got similar results. Since then modern neuro-science findings show that supportive interactions between children and their caretakers help construct and promote the maturation of the brains of the young. This science also shows that even with good support we are often asking them to do what they are not yet able to do because full maturation does not occur until they are in their 20s. Curiosity, impulsiveness, chance taking behavior, poor decision making, and more, can get young people with little support into trouble. And the response to trouble from authority figures in institutions is often control through punishment rather than to provide caring guidance that can enable the immature and underdeveloped child to learn and gain positive, useful competencies from the people around them. This process is much more difficult for the young who live in stressful environments to comprehend. It is a major reason why the school must be a supportive community.

Foreword

Early in my career I served on the Pardons Board for the state of Connecticut and I saw and heard the difficult stories of separation of the children of prisoners from their parents or caregivers. And the War on Drugs, zero tolerance discipline strategies, and other get tough on people approaches are now more harsh and devastating on families, contribute to a geometric progression of problem behaviors from generation to generation, increasing and intensifying the problems they are supposed to reduce. We must concentrate on prevention and reduction through the promotion of healthy community and family life. Diversion from the justice system, a focus on youth development and guidance, even de-criminalization of matters that are actually public health problems must occur along with the promotion of civility and preparation for life through school curriculum and activities intentionally designed to do so. We must eliminate the idea that arts and athletics, and other programs are "soft stuff", good for "our children", or the "gifted" but not for "them."

To be sure, we cannot save the world, not even all the children; even if we are supportive early in the life of each child and continue this to maturity. Our genetic predispositions, human nature, and an increasingly complex social system make this extremely difficult to impossible. But what we now call education and correction and/or punishment in our schools and penal systems are spectacular failures! And for historical reasons people of color are the greatest victims.

Most troublesome is the fact that there is strong evidence that the school wrapped in a community of caring, with well prepared educators, could make a significant difference. It could be designed in a way to strengthen families and communities and simultaneously enhance its primary functions of promoting development and academic learning. And most importantly, motivating and preparing the young to take responsibility for their own academic learning, behavior and preparation for adult life.

But most people, even deeply caring people, don't know that preparatory educator programs do not do much to prepare teachers and administrators to create school cultures that can support development, learning and a good foundation for adult life success. As late as 2010 a report based on a National Institute of Child Health and Human Development report indicated that 10% of educator preparation programs do not have a child development course requirement. Further, it showed that most of the 90% require only one such course, and 65% of those are taught outside the school of education. Little attention is given to the application of child principles in practice or how to create school communities that promote supportive cultures.

People, and the general public, have joined forces to undermine the justification for slavery, which was a major contributor to economic advantage and privilege, and moved a focus on test scores, rather than creating the rich and stimulating school experience that all children need, has been the case in modern school reform efforts. If my late mother could hear, that, today, they are grading teachers and schools without adequately preparing educators to teach and manage schools, she would shake her head in even greater dismay and would probably say, "No common sense". And she would be stunned by even the idea that educators could be prepared to do their jobs "on line"." And that is what they should expect" she would probably say if she could hear that 45% of all new teachers leave the field in five years.

But those of us concerned about the cradle to school to prison pipeline should expect more and demand more from state, local and national political, economic and social leaders responsible for the preparation of all children; particularly those whose families cannot provide what they need to have a chance to participate in the mainstream of American life without an education program geared to their needs. The message of this book is that it is less the people in prison as the problem and more the systems that we have allowed to ensnare them. And because racism is so ugly, pervasive and enduring and since we know that people of color are more often the victims, it is easy to focus on it as the underlying problem rather than a painful, powerful tactic. Throughout the history of the world people with power and privilege have used whatever possible to exploit and abuse the more vulnerable—from brute force, to varied claims of entitlement, to charges of inferiority and bad behavior—to maintain and justify their power and privilege. To America's credit, the vulnerable, many powerful people, and the general public, have joined forces to undermine the justification of slavery, a major contributor to economic disparity and privilege, and move us toward becoming a powerful economy and more just society.

But the rapid change in the nature of our economy and the failure to adjust our institutions fully enough and fast enough to make it possible for most of our young to participate in the mainstream of American life, caused us to leave too many people behind, and eventually in the underground rather than the mainstream economy. To maintain economic, political and social advantage and privilege, our society has used the tactic of blaming the victims rather than preventing the causes. A major reason that this has been possible is that we have been able to demonize the victims. The great value of this book is that it puts the face of mother, sister, husband and wife, rather than demons, on people who could and should be redirecting their own lives; caring for their children, and contributing to the well being of their communities and our country.

The book reminds us that mindless public policy is doing harm not only to the people in prison but to all of America, indeed, to the economic strength, vitality and hard fought for moral fiber of our country. We are already a less safe, open and grand society than we were just a generation ago. This is as much from internal shortcomings in policy as the external threat of terrorists. The plea of the author and the book is to make it possible for all of our young to have the opportunity to enjoy the fruits of our wealth, ingenuity, and commitment to justice. It is a plea for the good of us all.

We can do this.

James P. Comer, M.D., M.P.H

UPPER BUNKIES UNITE

PROLOGUE

The ultimate purpose of this book is to increase dialogue about the war on drugs, its relationship to the ills of over-incarceration, and its contribution to the destruction of families, particularly those in the black and brown populations. The priority is to encourage critical thinking about this country's policy of drug prohibition and incarceration and shed light on the over use of prisons and the need for a shift to community wellness.

I wrote this while serving a 24-month sentence in the federal prison for women in Danbury, Connecticut. I was sentenced for wire fraud in relation to my real estate law practice in Boston, Massachusetts. I wrote in response to the events, laws and policies being shaped on the outside by the Congress, local, state, and federal governments, the media, corporate boardrooms, sentencing reform organizations, the Federal Bureau of Prisons, the incarcerated and their families. These are my thoughts from atop a prison bunk and reflections from stories of the people within that prison and the issues that caused me to take pause and have something to say.

My goal is to raise awareness about the overuse of prisons and the failed war on drugs that keeps the prisons full at an annual cost of more than sixty nine billion dollars. I hope to create a more accurate portrait of the over two million adults and children warehoused in prisons in this country. I hope to encourage increased dialogue about the futility of the war on drugs and why it is necessary that the United States reconstruct our current criminal justice system to one of transformative, community justice.

Prior to going to federal prison I was just like many of you. I worked hard and paid my taxes. I had a family that I cared deeply for and children for whom I wanted the best education. I wanted to be safe and live in a healthy, thriving community. Even as a former criminal defense lawyer I didn't put much emphasis on the overall issue of the policy of a war on drugs, even though I considered myself to be a committed activist of sentencing reform and the advancement of social justice. Not long after walking into prison as an incarcerated person, I knew for sure that from that moment forward I had to use my voice to raise awareness among everyday people about mass incarceration as created by the war on drugs and that we must all organize, mobilize and coalition build with the one goal of ending this war. The war on drugs and mass incarceration has been the single leading cause of the breakdown and disenfranchisement of poor and predominantly black and brown communities. We must end this war. Just stop it. We must demand reallocation of the wasted tax dollars spent on enforcement and prisons and focus on decriminalization and legalization as the best alternatives for creating fair and successful drug policies that start with addressing the human needs of all impacted. And until we can accomplish that, we must encourage defendants to exercise their right to trial. We must force the system to grind to a halt from the weight of all the trial requests, engaging jury nullification to impede the flow of people into prisons while beginning a shift toward a restorative and transformative justice model in place of our current criminal justice system.

Prologue

During my work as a criminal defense lawyer I relied upon a lesson taught to me by attorney Yolanda Acevedo during my law school internship at the Massachusetts Public Defender Agency at Roxbury Defenders. The lesson was to always humanize our clients. Over the years, in many courtrooms, I saw this play out as defense lawyers concentrated on humanizing the person standing before the judge, as opposed to emphasizing the offense. In presenting the information in this book I chose to write from this same place because from the time I entered prison it was the human factor, the women behind the criminal labels who inspired me to write.

I invite readers to open their hearts and minds and join the dialogue about the need for a complete upheaval of our current criminal justice system from one of over-incarceration and wasted human potential, towards a focus on justice as healing.

INTRODUCTION

As a teenager during the late 70's and early eighties, I remember going to the old Roxbury district courthouse with a friend to support her brother who was a defendant in a criminal matter. In the old courthouse they used to bring the guys (It was always mostly all men back then) right up the front stairs of the courthouse to get them to the lockup on the top floor. So everyone, mothers, siblings, spouses, friends, would stand in a semi circle in the hallway waiting to hear all the commotion of the court officers bringing their loved ones, black men, chained together, handcuffs attached to waist irons, connected to leg restraints. The chains would clang and clatter as the guys, all hooked together, hopped in unison up each stair step so as not to fall over each other. As the tops of their heads appeared as they began their ascent, the awaiting group would squeeze a little closer, leaning forward and hoping to get a quick hello or message to let the guys know that someone came to see about them.

Once inside the courtroom we listened as the prosecutors described accused person after accused person as though they were all nothing but crazy, vicious people. Even as a very young person I knew that there was so much more to my friend's brother. We all loved him dearly and we looked up to him. He made sure we were safe outside and he was kind to us and always bought us all kinds of junk food from the corner store. I watched from the back of the courtroom and I felt a deep energy from this experience. A sense of suffering that I wanted to be a part of fixing. A truth that was missing that I wanted to be a part of telling. I decided that day I would become a criminal defense lawyer.

The Universe always has a way of correcting or realigning our path. Years after I sat with my friend in that courtroom, from the start of my pursuit of law as a profession there were many roadblocks and red flags. The first law school I attended I got into by the seat of my pants and had to move 1500 miles away to Florida with my then 6-year old daughter and no daycare. I was angry and sad even before leaving home as my boyfriend had just been sentenced and shipped off to a federal prison to serve a mandatory minimum for participating in selling cocaine.

No sooner than arriving at the Shepard Broad Law Center in Fort Lauderdale, we were practically blown back to Boston by hurricane Andrew. Not having experienced a hurricane before, I remember trying to figure out what to do and where to hide. My daughter, Ariel, and I first climbed into our bedroom closet. As the winds howled and the building began to shake, we crawled on our bellies to find shelter in our bathtub as was suggested by the news weatherman just before our power went out. This being the same bathroom I also used as a study room late at night so as not to wake my daughter while I tried to understand the Rule Against Perpetuity, fee simples and a whole lot of other not so simple legal stuff, in a bathtub. Somehow, on the night of Hurricane Andrew, between changing hiding places often, we weathered the storm.

A month later, just starting to recover from Andrew, a man decided to select our apartment to break into out of all the places in our sleepy little development. He walked up and kicked in our door and was standing looking crazy in our living room. And just as fast and smooth as he came in, my roommate, an ex-military wife and petite southern BAP, walked to her room and promptly returned brandishing a 45-caliber handgun. In her squeaky voice she calmly gave him a directive that went something like this: "Get out or I will blow your fucking head off." I think she said "motherfucker" too. The swearing was way over the top for her. I can't even comment about the gun. You think you know someone. Anyway, he left.

Besides hurricane Andrew and the crazy man, I remember a few significant things about that year. The first is the only time I remember laughing the entire time I was there. My torts law professor told us a joke to help us understand liability in reference to inherently dangerous activities such as eating eggs or driving a convertible car. "So what's next", he asked? "Will they soon make everyone wear helmets when driving with the top down?" I don't know if it was the pressure releasing suddenly or what, but I still think that image is one of the funniest things. It really was funny.

The second thing I remember with significance was going to work at the local Pep Boys auto supply store in Davie, Florida. The Klan still held rallies in Davie and often when we would come out of class we would find our cars papered with Klan propaganda. I showed up one day for my part time shift as a cashier, and was stopped in my tracks at the sight of the store flagpole that was now displaying the confederate flag. My days as an employee there were numbered.

Lastly, I went to dinner one evening at a mall with expensive boutique stores and restaurants. The weird thing was that the mall was named after a seriously resource deprived part of town that abutted the gated mall. As in raw sewage in the streets resource deprived. The street leading to the mall was lined with Florida style, low-rise public housing that seemed to be buckling from the Miami heat and the stench of the broken sewer lines. Once we made it through the gates of the mall, the scene changed dramatically. No offensive odors. The streets were well lit and people strolled along the outdoor mall area. Designer labels hung from signs over head, a far contrast from the old sneakers hanging by tattered shoelaces from the sagging electrical wires a few blocks away. Makeshift memorials of casualties of the drug war. I hobbled my way through that first year of law school and came limping back home to Boston with a GPA of about 1.0. The only option was starting over.

After returning to Boston and working for the Youth Advocacy Project at Roxbury Defenders, I eventually got accepted to Northeastern University School of Law. I was perfectly fine doing the work of the community liaison at the Youth Advocacy Project but I wanted to be a lawyer. Working under the direction of the now Honorable Judge Jay Blitzman and attorney Joshua Dohan provided me with the experience and credibility I needed to gain acceptance to Northeastern University School of Law. Unlike Florida, Northeastern University Law School was an amazing experience, albeit the red flags were still flying. One day I went to get some books from my locker and there was a note from the law school dean, David Hall. I went to his office and he sat me down and said "You certainly have the ability to be here, but I'm not sure that you have the ability to handle the access you will acquire to a world that few are allowed to enter… allowance into situations and places not open to most… I'm not sure that you will handle that well". Red flag. He was referring to me being headstrong and impatient. That I approached issues from a place of anger and blame. Something I continue to struggle with today. I was smart, but had no wisdom. I was eager for change but knew nothing about awareness and shifting out of the energy of struggle and suffering.

I operated from a place of emotional highjack. Daniel Goleman, author of Emotional Intelligence describes this as being at a point in evolution where we are able to negotiate our minds to think, plan, remember past events and organize things in our mind. These are all relatively new functions that our brains have evolved into doing over time. From the most primitive root, thc brain stem, emerged the emotional centers. Millions of years later in evolution, from these emotional areas evolved the thinning brain or 'neocortex.' The fact that the thinking brain grew from the emotional reveals much about the relationship of thought to feeling; there was an emotional brain long before there was a rational one.[i] Needless to say, mine, and a whole lot of others' are still developing. We are high jacked often by our emotions and when we do succumb to an impulsive act resulting in poor judgment, most of us wish we had made better choices.

Just as my law school dean warned me of the inequity between my academic versus my emotional intelligence, people in positions of power over the lives and freedom of others are no less vulnerable to the possibilities of emotional high jackings or behavior within the realm of inappropriate and deemed criminal. We've witnessed presidents in search of power, control and sexual gratification, suffer emotional high jackings leading to immoral and criminal behavior. We've seen it with judges who sentence countless people to prisons while engaging in the same acts in their personal lives. We see it with members of Congress who in emotionally and chemically intoxicated episodes commit all kinds of clandestine craziness involving drugs, alcohol, sexting, and then take the floor of the house and senate and in broad brush strokes create laws that clearly dismiss the human factor involved in the individual's actions. Laws such as one-size fits all mandatory minimum and guideline sentences.

I was incarcerated with a woman who was a first-time, nonviolent offender convicted of embezzlement and sentenced to serve 60 months, a most common federal guideline sentence. The former chief judge for the Northern District of Georgia had sentenced her. He had been appointed to the bench by President Ronald Reagan in 1987 and took senior status in 2008. According to court documents, at the time the judge was presiding over the woman's case, he was involved in his own malfeasance. Later, the judge was charged with possession of cocaine, marijuana and the painkiller oxicodone. He was also charged with possessing a firearm as an unlawful user of controlled substances and aiding and abetting the possession of drugs by his female companion. There were many women in the prison I was in who had years added to their sentences as an enhancement for a firearm being on the premises where they were arrested. That firearm enhancement at sentencing also makes them ineligible for sentence reductions and some rehabilitative and second-chance opportunities during their incarceration that most of them would otherwise be eligible for, adding years to the time they are warehoused in prison.

In the judge's case, he was sentenced to 30 days in federal prison and 400 hours of community service, resigned his judicial post and surrendered his law license. Based on the federal sentencing guidelines, he could have received a sentence of more than four years, which was the amount of time agreed to in his original plea deal and more in line with the numerous, lengthy federal prison sentences he handed down over more than a decade of sitting on the bench. I raise this case to help illustrate the point about the importance of the human factor in determining appropriate sentencing, for all defendants. I remember reading the Washington Post article about the judge's case with my friend in Danbury who he sentenced and thinking how deserving of such a sentence she was and how crazy it was that she had to be locked up in Danbury until 2016. Not to mention that the victims of her financial offense certainly were not going to receive any restitution while she was forced to work for the Federal Bureau of Prisons making on average 12 cents an hour. Maybe while the judge was in federal prison for 30 days he came to understand the waste of human potential in warehousing people, very much like himself, in prisons for unreasonably long periods of time that is not restorative to any party or cost effective for taxpayers.

Hard on crime policy has moved us into a zero tolerance mode. We've become a society that looks first for how we can fit a person's actions into a criminal penalty solely for the purpose of punishment and incarceration. Considering an offender's individual circumstances only applies to the important or worthy members of society. The result has been that the United States has more people and a higher percentage of the population locked up than any other country. There are currently more than two million people currently in prison. One in thirty nine adults in this country are under some form of control by a criminal justice agency. The incarceration rate for women has increased by four hundred percent. The increase has been eight hundred percent for African American women. More than two and a half million children have one or both parents in prison and studies demonstrate that sixty eight percent of those children will have contact with the juvenile justice system.

Predominantly African Americans are casualties of this country's war on drugs. It has depleted every available resource for educating our children and providing healthcare, employment and affordable housing to not only poor people, but now to many in the middle class across racial lines. Most troubling is the steady erosion of the hard won civil rights advancements by the race-based disenfranchisement legislation promulgated by the crafters of the war on drugs and blindly accepted by mainstream America.

This attempt at writing is my contribution to the movement to stop our hysterical, fear and race-based high jacking of our intelligence about what crime is versus a public health dilemma and poverty. This is about raising awareness and a call to dismantle down to the very core our criminal justice system. As a collective community, facing a collective karma, we all stand guilty of keeping in place such a tragic, inhumane and unjust system.

NOT THAT SIMPLE

I know that most people who haven't experienced being a participant in the criminal justice system, including anything to do with prisons, probably don't think much about what I have to say. We feel like there are so many more worthy causes to expend our time, energy and often money on. I don't have the money of the Koch brothers to put my message into the psyches of the American people, nor the political clout of groups like the American Legislative Exchange Council and the corporate interests they promote. The sentiment is that you had an opportunity, a choice like everyone else, to not do whatever crime you committed that landed you at the mercy of the system and in prison. So even if the system is damaged or desperately flawed and in need of reform, so what? If you can't do the time, don't do the crime. It's that simple.

But it's not that simple when you consider that the time is not based reasonably on the offense. It's not that simple because incarceration, warehousing people in prison, has most often become the answer to all crimes and defendants, regardless of individual intent and circumstances.

It's not that simple because instead of a system created to address the root causes of behavior we have spiraled into a system created to address the need and greed of politics and a prison industry built to serve political aspirations with a hard-on-crime platform that has perpetuated misplaced fear among voters. A fear that has been used to glue us to our television sets and brainwash us into being sold more and more material junk and false politics.

It's not that simple when the sentencing laws are grossly overly harsh and disproportionately dispensed based on race and class resulting in a prison industry that has removed a huge segment of surplus labor, mostly black men, from our innercities. Instead of putting money into education for children and infrastructure job opportunities to invest in our future and collective prosperity as a country, we have re-directed dollars to support a failed drug war and expanding prison system.

In as few as twenty years, even though the country's crime rate has decreased overall, our prison population has soared multiple times. Mostly first-time, nonviolent offenders, comprise sixty percent of our prison population. Most of these offenders are serving protracted, unreasonably long sentences for minor roles in drug possession and distribution. Politicians have cushioned their seats of power with a "hard-on-crime mantra, using crack cocaine as a foundation for creating racist and classist sentencing guidelines and mandatory minimum sentencing that have resulted in a turn-style type of prisonization for millions of poor people of color and their children. Reallocation of resources from social programs to prisons has created the stranglehold of constant surveillance and presence of police authority in poor communities where constitutional rights are abused and eroded to non-existence for many.

It's not that simple when women are now being incarcerated in far greater numbers than ever experienced in history and it's not that simple when over two million children in this country have one or both parents in prison. Countless studies have determined how devastating the impact is on children when their mothers are incarcerated. And it's not that simple when the money to educate those children has been reallocated to fund prisons, creating a school to prison pipeline for the children left behind.

And it's not that simple when underfunded reentry programs, harsh employment and housing barriers and distorted public perception make it almost impossible for formerly incarcerated people to gain life-sustaining opportunities.

And it's not that simple when states' voting disenfranchisement laws strip offenders of their right to vote, completing a circle of severe punishment and on-going, generational prisonization.

If you do not think this affects you, think again. As I mentioned, sixty percent of the current prison population are first-time, nonviolent offenders. Minor tax evasion will send you to federal prison for six months to a year. Just one day in prison can change your life forever. In the federal prison camp where I served my twenty four-month sentence, in addition to the majority black women serving drug sentences, a large number of white, middle class women where serving sentences for financial and tax offenses. The United States incarcerates more people than any other country in the world, regardless of the numerous studies that demonstrate the futility of over-incarceration and its negative impact on society as a whole. Still we create more and more unreasonable sentences and incarcerate more and more people. It's not that simple. I hope in reading this book you will begin to open your mind and if possible, your heart enough to at least join a discussion about the criminal justice policies of our country.

SELF SURRENDER

I was sentenced to the lowest security federal prison called a prison camp. I was eligible to self-surrender. I remember that drive with my husband, children and parents. We rented a mini van so we could all fit in one car for the drive. I sat in the back seat with my 6 month old son and 13-year old daughter. My husband and adult daughter were in the front and my parents huddled together in the middle row. As a family we had taken many road trips and I found myself at times drifting off and momentarily forgetting the destination of this one. When we got lost a few times I called the prison for directions. It still felt more like the many times I called a hotel from the road to let them know we'd be checking in a little late.

I showed up to the prison on the designated date and checked myself in. That was the end of any sensible reality. You enter a world where nothing makes sense. You're kept removed from society but with society all around you. The outside world bombards you during your time in prison. It's not like the old days when guards came to work with an old tin lunch pail and thermos. The modern day officers come clutching Coach bags, big gulp Slurpee drinks and coffee from Dunkin Donuts. Just a few days prior to coming to prison you couldn't start your day without that same cup of Dunkin coffee.

Once I had said my goodbyes to my family and they were directed out of the prison lobby, I was sent into a large holding cell within a secure area. One of the things you encounter when you enter prison is the first of many strip searches. I've come to believe that the process is not so much to actually find contraband, but to establish that you have been stripped of your previous life and now are under the control of the prison. Your first and last strip search is a demoralizing, humiliating, intrusive experience. That same woman you passed in the coffee shop parking lot just before surrendering is now barking orders at you to take your clothes off and what part of your clothes did you think didn't also include your bra and panties? The area where the strip search takes place is not usually a place where you want to be naked.

There I stood butt naked in a stall experiencing my first strip search in the receiving and delivery section of the women's federal prison in Danbury, Connecticut, still kind of expecting the officer to give me something to put under my bare feet. Her blank stare told me otherwise. Shake out your hair. Open your mouth. Stick out your tongue. Lift your arms over your head. Lift your breasts. Turn around. Bend. Spread your butt cheeks. Cough. I still don't understand why they make us spread our cheeks and cough. We're women. We have choices. The butt hole is not the first place we would choose to stuff something. Not to mention we hold in babies, tampons penises, pee pee. So right away you start to recognize the inefficiencies of a poorly designed system.

Finally I was processed along to another area where more mug shots of me were taken and photos of my tattoos. This time I was with a very kind officer who said he would hurry and get me processed so that I could be sent up to the camp and not be stuck in the segregated housing unit, called the S.H.U., or the hole. It was late Friday afternoon and all the staff was hustling to get out of there for the weekend. Had it not been for his kindness I would have been stuck in the hole for the weekend, if not longer. I came to know Mr. B as one of the most respected officers at the prison. Some months later when I saw him I thanked him for his compassion toward me during my intake. His response was that he answered to a higher power that instilled in him a responsibility to treat people with kindness and dignity. Mr. B was one of the first officers I met upon arrival and the last one to discharge me when it was time to leave. I am still grateful to him for his kindness on my first day.

I was glad to hear that I had been designated to the camp. It is on the same grounds as the prison, but it's different. It's lower security. You're not behind the barbed-wire fence and you're not locked in cells and can move around inside and outside the perimeter of the building.

In the beginning it was hard to believe that I had wound up there. I cried a lot, quietly. Three days had passed and I hadn't been able to call my husband and children. I was told that two women, a counselor and a case manager, oversaw the day-to-day administration of the prison camp. I met the case manager during my intake but had not seen her since or met the counselor. I couldn't make a phone call until the counselor provided me with something called a PAC number and a PIN number and then I needed to make sure I had money in my commissary account to purchase phone minutes. The other women told me that the counselor took her time providing new women with this information. So there I sat and waited. Day after day, having had no contact with my family since they watched me walk into the prison. The other thing the women told me was not to ask the counselor anything.

When you come in as the "new girl" you have a couple of ways of being assisted by the women. The first thing people do is relate to you by your race, black, Latino, white, Asian. With me, the women told me that they couldn't really tell. The second way people relate to you and may want to help you out is based on where you're from. So the first group to reach out to me was the white women from my hometown of Boston. Wendy and Rita. Rita was from the predominantly Irish- catholic neighborhood of South Boston, Southie, as we Bostonians refer to it, and I liked being with her because she sounded like home. These women would remain my friends for my entire stay at Danbury and still today. They provided me with necessary start-up supplies like a real bar of soap and some toothpaste. Most importantly, Rita gave me a pen, paper and a stamped envelope to send word home to my family that I was ok while I waited for the day whenever the counselor felt like providing me what I needed to make a telephone call.

Eventually, as word got around that I was from Boston, some Latina women from Jamaica Plain, MA, a neighborhood near mine, brought me a few pieces of clothing, T-shirts, shorts and a clean pair of underwear. I had come in on a Friday afternoon and I was not dressed out, or provided a change of prison uniform or underwear until that following Tuesday. So to receive these things from the women was a big deal. Eventually I received a box of items from some of the Black women who told me they thought I was Latina.

Almost immediately upon arrival I realized the monotony was enough to drive a person crazy. It was just like the movie, Ground Hog day. I kept replaying how I drove myself up with my family, walked up to the front desk in the lobby and told the officer, “I’m here to self-surrender.” Such an awkward thing to say. They stripped searched me, put me in some pajama looking uniform and sent me on up the hill to the camp. And there I sat. I decided to begin writing down my thoughts.

The prison jobs were menial and brain dead. Still, most women wanted to go to work everyday because it was the only thing that helped the time go by. Sometimes though some would come up with the best excuses I’ve ever heard to get out of work. Like the “I’ve got a no prolonged standing” excuse. We all used this from time to time mostly during blizzards when they would toss us all out of bed at four in the morning and make us shovel in the blinding snow.

After months of having a work assignment in the prison garage I was fortunate to land one of the few teaching positions. I taught English and science G.E.D. classes and an English as a second language class. Thankfully because of this for a few hours everyday I was engaged in doing something fulfilling for me and something that was helping the other women. The women were invested in getting their General Equivalency Diplomas yet even after being there for years many would still leave there undereducated and unskilled. One day my friend Sally, I called her Sally-Girl. I don't know why. When we would pass by one another she would always say, "Hello Andrea Goode-James." And I would always respond, "Hello Sally-Girl." One day she said to me, "I got a restitution bill of one million dollars and they put me in prison, paid for by the taxpayers, to just sit around. I am paid 25 cents an hour to wash the prison vehicles and maybe, maybe, I might come out of here five years later with a certificate in crocheting." But let me tell you something. Nobody could clean the prison vehicles like Sally-Girl. It was like meditation to her. Sally also had the nicest All-American son whose activities in the United States Navy I followed. I was so happy for Sally the times he was on leave and would come to visit his mother. He was such a great young man and so handsome in his uniform. He made sure he came to see his mom. I would always ask Sally to describe to me what ocean in the world he was stationed on in a United States Naval ship somewhere.

I would often wonder how many of the women would make it on the outside after years of being away and losing everything. Children they have to figure out how to pull back together, love, teach, raise, feed, clothe. How do you make it with little to nothing, after being shut away and disconnected for so long? The women in the camp drove vehicles, trucks, snow plows and transported food and supplies across the grounds. There was even a town driver prison job. She would transport women upon their release all over Connecticut, New York and even New Jersey to the bus and train stations and airports but she couldn't go home. Warehoused often for years in this federal prison, kept away from her children although often she drove past the very neighborhood her family lived in.

There was a nine-month drug treatment program. But most of the women locked up for using and selling drugs were doing way more than a year, which would be a reasonable time for a drug program lasting 9 months. These women were serving ten, twenty year, mandatory minimum sentences. Everyday-people caught up while trying to figure out daily survival.

So we sat. Most of us having made a mistake, after entire life times of playing by the rules, raising our families, walking a straight line, voting, PTA meetings, volunteering, feeding the hungry and clothing the homeless. Never an act of violence toward anyone. Prayed in our churches, mosques, masjids, synagogues and meditation groups. Managed to figure out how to make it to the next day. Struggled to get an effective education plan for our child. Held out hope that he was learning in an overcrowded, underfunded school. Then, in addition to all that struggle, the women were taken from their children's lives because of the choices left them in trying to keep it all together. Falling into traps of illegal behavior in efforts to enable a normal existence. Those were the majority of the women I was in prison with. Everyday-people. Kind and caring people serving unreasonably long sentences for choices made trying to exist as ordinary people with too few resources.

I read a book while I was in there titled, The Universe in a Nutshell. It's by the famous scientist, Stephen Hawkins. He's compared to scientists like Einstein. Anyway, there was a picture in the book, thankfully, that demonstrated how space is not a solid; or rather it showed that matter causes the weight of things to bend even the empty outer spaces of the universe. So for instance the weight of the sun causes an impression in the universe that causes other things of less weight to be drawn in by the energy created by the matter of the thing. That's how life can be sometimes for everyday-people. The heaviness of other things draws us into other realms.

Not only aren't educational and skills training opportunities available in prison commensurate with the years of warehousing a person, but there is no awareness or trauma intervention training. Nothing is offered to raise our awareness of the materialism and corporate greed that too often gets us in trouble in the first place. That toxicity of the corporate world is now so pervasive that it is even seeping into the womb and polluting the blood streams of our unborn fetuses. Nothing is offered to people in prison to make us aware of and slow down the incessant whirring of their ego voices. The stuff that self-help books talk about. Nothing to help us develop a practice of shifting our overall response to things. Nothing to help us understand that we have choices as to how to respond to the events and emotions experienced. Nothing to help us learn that bad feelings, anger, jealousy, insecurity are not who we truly are, but are feelings that come and go. There is little to introduce incarcerated people to that inner shift away from the falsities of life to the truth of who we are. Prison only exacerbates the negative stuff that we constantly see and hear about ourselves.

Shifting our mind and our spirit takes being introduced to change. It takes practice and with practice comes more awareness. It's like losing weight. When I started working out and losing weight, that weight didn't just fall off overnight. Over time it melted off like that big pile of snow left over from the big storm that refuses to go away. It melts slowly, in rolling layers leaving a pile of debris that needs to be cleaned up. So too all the junk that we carry around that can lead us to prison. This is justice as healing. It is helping people to reach that place of awareness. Prison doesn't provide that. For most of the prison population, like most people on the outside, awareness and healing is what we need.

INCARCERATION POLITICS

I was born in 1964 into a family of educator activists. My parents, uncles, aunts and grandparents are intelligent people. I grew up in the Sugar Hill section of Roxbury, Massachusetts, where we have a richness of black life and activist energy. Sugar Hill was what my parents' generation called it, we just referred to our neighborhood as "up off Humboldt Ave." Growing up, my uncle told me stories about his childhood friend, Eugene, who sang beautifully and played the violin and became the man, Louis Farrakhan, and about the boy who became the man, Malcolm X. My grandmother, a community legend, was one of the first black nurses to break the color barrier in Boston hospitals. She always said that she entered through the back door of nursing and came out the front door as a public health nursing supervisor. At 65, she retired from public health nursing and went on to become a filmmaker and videographer, documenting the lives of black centenarians she referred to as unsung heroes. As a child I would go with my grandmother to help with her interviews. It was my job to hold the tape recorder and microphone while she did the filming. The common theme in all the life stories she captured was great accomplishment notwithstanding great struggle.

Like the natural course of learning to speak English, I heard the language of black struggle, community advocacy and academic achievement. As a child I never remember hearing my parents argue, but I do remember listening to them on Sunday mornings talking over breakfast about social and political issues with such passion that I sometimes confused this discourse as arguing. My mother would say, "We're not arguing. We're having a discussion." My parents spoke the language of intellectuals and although I often did not understand what their words meant, I knew from the energy of the conversation they were talking about the struggle for the advancement of black people.

Every wall in our home was covered with shelves with books. Titles like *Black Like Me, My Brother's Keeper, and Psychology of the Black Child.* Hearing my parents' conversations and seeing the community work they were involved in were the seeds planted in me that started my mother telling me from a small child that I couldn't social work the entire neighborhood.

In college I majored in English and studied black history. I celebrated black people as the director of the black student center. As college students we went out into our community of Roxbury and organized. At that time we were organizing young people involved in what was being called "gang and drug" activity. Crack cocaine had been added to the list of drugs being sold and used and the legislators and the Clinton Administration weren't wasting any time enacting meaner and lengthier drug sentencing laws, while providing billions of dollars to build more prisons and increase police presence in urban communities.

From coast to coast, black communities were flooded with what seemed like an inexhaustible supply of crack cocaine, or "work", as it was referred to by the once chronically unemployed, but soon to be dangerously and illegally employed, young black men and women involved in the drug trade. As economist Manny Marable described, the cycle of destruction starts with chronic, mass unemployment and poverty. Real incomes for the majority of the working poor actually fell significantly during Clinton's second term in office. After the 1996 welfare act, the Great Society era's social safety net was largely pulled apart. As the Bush administration took power, chronic joblessness spread to Black workers in the manufacturing sector. By early 2004, in cities such as New York, fully one-half of all Black male adults were outside of the paid labor force.[ii]

The prisons started to fill up and remain over-capacity, with people serving 10, 15, 25, and life sentences for selling drugs. Sentences for crack cocaine were the most severe, resulting in defendants receiving decades long sentences for a one-hundredth of the amount it would take to receive the same sentence for powder cocaine. This is what the struggle had come to now. As people already embroiled in the daily struggle for quality of life issues, employment, housing, health care and education, now a deluge of crack cocaine assaulted the black community. The new voices of the struggle were our voices trying to organize in our communities through a dense haze of fear re-generated by tough-on-crime political rhetoric and media images using crack babies and crack-related sensationalized crime stories. Poverty issues were lost in the political fist pumping for containment and a war on drugs invoking saturated police presence and the laws to remove and warehouse people for years in newly built prisons.

Twenty years later, after college, law school and years of public interest work and private law practice, I was sentenced to federal prison under a federal sentencing guideline that required me to serve time for mail and wire fraud. I walked into a prison system crammed full of casualties of the drug war. It was here for the first time that I truly understood the struggle. I had life experiences from birth that shaped my interests and commitments and I chose my profession as a criminal defense lawyer based on those same things. And it was those same interests and commitments to be a part of activism and change on behalf of my people that brought me to federal prison. I was naïve and misguided certainly. But I have learned much on the road of my rebellion.

It was in prison that I saw crystal clear the stuff that my parents were talking about. It was there that I saw the warehousing of poor black and brown people, as a result of not only the stepped up war on drugs, but reaching further in the past to the backlash from the 1960s civil rights movement and the liberal Warren Supreme Court's overturning of conservative criminal justice policies. The concept of the war on drugs was born of the 1960s civil rights protest era. In a response to the feeling of the powerful, wealthy, political right that the country was swinging too far to a liberal, socially conscious society. The Goldwater – Nixon era launched a calculated and nefarious campaign of fear-based propaganda to convince Middle America that the country was under siege by criminals and if something wasn't done, they would take over the country. A war on crime became the mantra for the conservative right to secure votes. A cabal of leading industrialists, along with the right-wing journalist William f. Buckley, met to develop strategies to turn the tide. Wealthy Americans contributed funds to create "think tanks" that promulgated the conservative ideology and the power elite formed political action committees (PACs) that infused the political campaigns of conservatives with massive sums of money.[iii] While in prison I came to truly understand the words of political prisoners like Angela Davis, Safiya Bukhari, Kamau Sadiki and Susan Rosenberg and their life-long commitments to the advocacy for the rights of the oppressed. And I understood clearly that for my generation, as well, it included those serving drug sentences. The legacy of the black panthers, Safiya, and the men and women killed or still incarcerated today, some 30 years later, in federal prisons, for their political beliefs. But, so too does political prisoner include the crack cocaine and drug defendants. Those sentenced to years of imprisonment under the 100:1 crack to powder cocaine disparity, voted in by a United States Congress swept up in the politics of prisons and warehousing the poor. Prisoners of unreasonably long state and federal mandatory minimum and guideline drug sentences that were the result of politics aimed at removing the very focus of the original political prisoners, the very people our freedom fighters hoped to educate and liberate.

We must challenge ourselves to openly acknowledge the lengths the United States has gone and will go to thwart efforts for progress of social movements within this country. In 1968 the government used hostile programs and propaganda to thwart the civil rights movement. Covert domestic operations such as COINTELPRO, were used to stamp out social progress. In COINTELPRO, J. Edgar Hoover, the first Director of the Federal Bureau of Investigations, gave authority to the F.B. I. to use any manner of activities in order to destroy the black liberation movements in the country, even if they had to manufacture evidence or charges. A constant barrage of fear-filled media propaganda twisted the progressive message of the black liberation and Native American movements into hostile, violent acts of terrorism. Social movements for basic human rights became synonymous with crime. It wasn't until the results of the 1973 Church Committee Hearings, chaired by Senator Frank Church (D-Idaho), that the truth about COINTELPRO and the tactics of the F.B.I. and United States intelligence activities were acknowledged. Tactics that destroyed the people movements built with principles articulated in the United Nations Universal Declaration of Human Rights that helped shape missions such as free breakfast programs, voter registration drives, politics schools, clothing drives and programs to support the education of inner-city children. These same quality of life human issues are the lures of the inner-city drug trade as most whom are involved make that choice to earn just enough money to pay rent and feed and clothe their family.

The problems are multiple. There is an available source of income in the form of an apparently inexhaustible supply and demand commodity such as cocaine. There are next to no jobs, and no other regular and consistent, quality of life sustaining economic opportunities for many. Still children go to bed hungry. The majority of the poor in this country are small children who are not only chronically hungry, but also homeless. I can't leave out those who create "work" out of selling drugs from those deemed political prisoners. Politics is not for the poor. Politics is a vehicle to sustain the middle class consumerism that upholds the capitalism that created and shapes this country. Politics has used the poor and the collateral issues of poverty to separate and devalue those who have not made it out of poverty to join the middle class. And harsh laws and policies have been enacted to deal with people who are poor. This is why I say those who fall into the traps of drug selling, for instance, are also political prisoners.

Afghanistan is the largest supplier of opium to the United States, while within the United States, domestic policy continues to sustain a war on drugs. For millions of people in and outside of the United States, whether it's the street corner dealer or the Southeast Asian opium farmer, or the Columbian coca farmer, the drug trade is the only thing providing an economy. And the demand for those drugs is great not just in the United States, but also in China, Japan, and Europe. Most fatal is the role that U.S. drug policies have played in mass incarceration leading to the destruction of families, the displacement of children and the systematic erosion of basic civil rights. The war on drugs continues everyday to be at the head of the policies in this country that maintain power in the hands of the few while maintaining oppressive, often deadly control of the poor and people of color.

Throughout my prison sentence I made several requests to friends and family for books and research material. My dear friends Betty Burkes and Catherine Hoffman sent me tons of books, many of them generously provided by Barry Phillips, a professor and long time activist. Barry's book donations literally helped start a movement in Danbury.

Among the offerings was Dr. Ruth Wilson Gilmore's book, Golden Gulag: Prisons, Surplus, Crisis, and Opposition in Globalizing California. This book became one of the most important to my education and research. Dr. Ruth Wilson Gilmore is a professor and a leading anti-prison activist. Her book analyzes the economic and political changes leading to the expanse of prisons in California. It was Dr. Gilmore's book that we used in Danbury to teach us how to shape our issues and organize. As a result of reading Golden Gulag, we started our organization, Families for Justice as Healing, from inside the prison.

One day during mail call I received a packet from my dad containing a copy of President Dwight D. Eisenhower's 1961 farewell speech when he first referred to the term "military industrial complex" and warned the American people of the threat it posed to the nation. Included in the envelope was also a transcript of an interview a journalist, Trevor Paglen, had with Dr. Ruth Gilmore. It was titled, From Military Industrial Complex To Prison Industrial Complex, and in it she talks about how the military industrial complex had a cultural effect on this country to constantly refresh, renew, and reinvigorate the cultural violence that holds this country together. To have this kind of military industrial complex, you have to justify it by having a society that always imagines itself at war with someone else.[iv] Dr. Gilmore likens the military industrial complex to a prison industrial complex and states that in the 1980s and 1990s, the United States prison system numbers hit record high after high, year after year. More and more states and counties built more and more prisons, passed more and more mandatory minimum sentencing laws, and these massive prison systems and severe sentencing laws became totally normal. A lot of people were able to see that it had all of the complexities of the military industrial complex, and began talking about a prison industrial complex.[v]

The same concept of building an economy based on war was the same concept behind extending the meaning of war to include domestic policies that control surplus labor and build an economy grounded by a drug war and mass incarceration. Creating a worldwide military presence to stay on top of the global competition to this country's dominance and capitalistic endeavors requires an international presence. This is needed for the U.S. to continue developing intelligence through covert, secretly funded operations. Often these allies are the same countries that have a drug product in abundance that there is a considerable demand for in this country. Just as we now know that cocaine, heroin and guns were traded to fund government covert operations during the secret wars of the C.I.A. that were waged in Central America, Iran and Libya during the 1980s, negotiations for intelligence still has allowed turning a blind eye to international drug traffickers who are the sources of valuable intelligence information. The money generated from the international drug and gun trade help fund covert operations and build personal and political profit and a military industrial complex rivaled now only by its counterpart, a criminal justice – prison industrial complex.

This is a result of the drug trade that is never fully discussed. We have been silenced by mainstream opinion. It is shaped by media messages that shift the focus to show black men in the U.S. as dangerous and violent drug dealers. There is also political hard-on-crime rhetoric that causes even conscious, thinking people to avoid exploring the reality of the seeds of economic growth planted by the drug trade. Selling drugs provides income. To state this is not in support of selling drugs. It is an effort to show the importance of taking a close look at the many sides of the drug trade. It is to highlight all of the motivations behind it, including what it could produce minus the illegality. What economic opportunities could be available in poor urban communities?

Notwithstanding its controversy there is much to be learned about what that stream of income, or specifically, the taxation and regulation of drug sales, could provide. Not to mention the huge impact that decriminalization or legalization would have on increasing resources for drug treatment, education, and harm reduction alternatives to incarceration.

Once drugs make the way to the streets of the U.S., the same entrepreneurial maneuvering used by the world's intelligence agencies is employed on the street level and it is that upward economic mobility that the U.S. drug war is designed to eradicate. The concept of using the drug trade as a pillar of our international and domestic intelligence does not translate well for those in power as applied to the domestic drug trade. Like the government intelligence agencies, black men, in their own organizations, began to realize the power of using drug proceeds in their own struggle for upward mobility. That same entrepreneurial spirit on the street level, combined with a drive of people to overcome adversity, as young, aggressive street level dealers began joining forces and organizing their efforts to build businesses and legitimate streams of revenue from drug sales proceeds in resource deprived neighborhoods.

The passage of the Anti-drug Abuse Act of 1986 was the law that instituted the crack/powder sentencing differential and created the basic structure of federal mandatory minimums for drug trafficking.[vi] A driving force behind these provisions was the powder cocaine overdose of basketball star Len Bias, which prompted a remarkable level of media attention and a moral panic about not powder, but crack cocaine.[vii] The Anti-Drug Abuse bill was pushed forward and enacted without hearings or input from experts. Some lawmakers conceded that the legislation attempted to appease an electorate that had become hysterical over an alleged epidemic of crack cocaine, which was fed in part by inflammatory claims about the drug.[viii] For voters the perceived crises centered again, as in 1965, on ensuring that the rebellious surplus population was contained. A new form of social control was born as well as a new form of revenue for middle class Americans. Many ex-military personnel were now employed via the massive expansion of the prison system. The prison industrial complex was now supporting the military industrial complex.

In 1994, President Bill Clinton signed the most expensive federal crime bill in history into law. The law allocated almost 24 billion dollars to enable local law enforcement agencies to add 100,000 new police officers and 7.9 billion dollars to construct new state prisons. Again, In Clinton's 1999 state of the union message, crime took center stage as he promised to provide funds for an additional 60,000 police officers. There were, of course, strings attached to these funds: State and municipal governments had to agree to follow federal sentencing guidelines, including mandatory minimum sentences, which spread like wildfire across the country with state legislation crafted by the American Legislative Exchange Council and its major funder, the NRA. During Clinton's presidency the allocation of funds for our war on drugs tripled, and the severity of sentences for even possession of minor amounts of drugs soared.[ix] The government started pouring huge amounts of money into enforcement and prisons, an amount now totaling in excess of sixty nine billion dollars per year. The push was on and somehow we became matter-of-fact about protracted prison sentences.

The stories always seemed to sneak up on me. I would be sitting and talking or walking around the prison track with someone. I heard the amount of time they were doing. It was 312 months, 180 months or 120 months. The feds give it to you in months. I guess because initially it was difficult for them to even justify the sentence handed down in years.

These sentences were metered out to first-time, non-violent offenders. They were given to people who had never been arrested before, never even so much as a parking ticket. The length of the sentences are staggering and the stories never got old about what the moment was like when that person first realized that they would be stuck in prison for many, many years.

Easter described it best when she told us about hearing the judge say her sentence. Janet Easter was the cook at Danbury for most of the time that I was there. She was finally released after serving a seventeen-year drug sentence. She said that at her sentencing the judge said something about so many months and she was sitting there trying to understand what he was talking about because she didn't understand what he was saying in regards to 204 months. She just started crying and looking back at her family and trying to get her head clear enough to figure out how many years were 204 months. She could see her family digging through purses and pockets trying to produce a pen and paper. Finally her brother started making hand gestures to her and mouthing 17 years.

I was in prison with women whom have been in a prison for decades for non-violent drug offenses. And there are still, today, young women coming into prison everyday just beginning mandatory minimum and guideline drug sentences, for unreasonably long 10 or 15-year sentences. I met older women, like Phyllis Hardy, "Grandma", who is currently on her 22nd year of a 30-year sentence for selling cocaine. At 70 years old she needs a knee replacement and struggles everyday to walk herself across the prison yard to her job at UNICOR. Still after being locked up for 22 years she is not a candidate for any form of early release. There is no federal parole. It was eliminated with the onset of mandatory minimums. We pray everyday that her plea for her commutation is granted by the President and U.S. Pardon

Attorney, or at the very least, the Federal Bureau of Prisons will approve the knee replacement she has been waiting years for.

These long sentences are not just for crack or heroin anymore, but also for methamphetamine, prescription drugs, and even marijuana. And still there remains an unjustifiable, scientifically unsupported disparity in sentencing between crack and powder cocaine, after Congress' recent adjustment from a one hundred percent disparity to eighteen percent.

More than twenty-five years after mandatory minimum and harsh, unreasonably long guideline sentences have been in effect, the United States has replaced social justice advancements with crippling, punitive drug laws resulting in mass incarceration with no end to the demand for drugs in this country. This is so even as the crime rate has decreased. Surely the term political prisoner includes the millions serving time under these laws. At the time of the final edit of this book I received a letter from Phyllis Hardy "Grandma". Her most recent application to President Obama and the United States Pardon Attorney, for commutation of her sentence, had been denied.

LOSING MY TICKET

I got hit in my head really hard three times in my life that I can remember. The first time I was ice-skating. I wasn't very good. I was in elementary school and I attended a private school that had its own skating rink. In the early afternoons there was free skate and at the end of the free skate session the varsity hockey team would come barreling onto the ice. They were a menacing sight and their speed made it feel like flying torpedoes suddenly surrounded you. That day was no different. As the hockey players started their practice I couldn't walk-skate myself off of the ice fast enough. I spun around on wobbly ankles and fell head first onto the ice. A huge knot instantly appeared on my forehead and I still have a hard spot on my head where I made contact with the ice.

I should have known that there was something wrong with me then because even though I was in excruciating pain and had hit the ice so hard that I think I passed out, still I didn't want my friend's mother to think I got hurt on her watch. I made up a big story that I had received the huge, purple, pulsating knot sometime before. They must have thought I was really crazy because it was clear that it was a fresh wound, not to mention that I had spent the entire afternoon with them with no humungous bump on my forehead.

The second time my head was hit was when I was around 11 years old and my father took me, my older brother and my sisterfriend, Kass, to a beach somewhere. We hadn't intended on going to the beach. It was just something like we were driving, saw a beach and got out to look at the water and skip a few rocks or something. The tide was out and the exposed shore stretched deep back from the top of the dry part of the sand, exposing slick rocks dimpling the shore.

Even though I stood just a few feet in front of him, my brother started throwing rock missiles whizzing past my head into the water. First a small one. Then a bigger one coming closer to my head. Then a massive rock clunked me on the back of my head right where the scalp begins to indent to meet up with the spine. I can still remember hearing the muted thud from inside my head when the rock hit. The rock hit me with such bulls eye precision that I knew he meant to hit me. That's when we should have known that there was something wrong with him too.

The third time was when I was 15 and nothing short of experiencing a period of for sure mental illness, far surpassing everyday adolescence. I was riding in a car with a crazy man that I barely knew but somehow thought was ok to ride around with. Looking back on that day it's so easy to understand how adolescents can unintentionally get into serious trouble under the influence of some adults. This guy paced around like he was high all the time and couldn't keep still. They say God looks out for babies and fools and that day I was both. No sooner than we pulled off in the car he drove into an intersection without stopping, was hit in the rear by an oncoming car and we fishtailed into a stone wall. My head slammed into and cracked the car windshield.

Years later I read an article that explained how a head injury could cause a person to do dumb things. This didn't escape me when it finally hit me that I had been juggling over a million dollars of money belonging to some of the banks I represented as a real estate conveyance attorney. Why the three head injuries came to mind I have no idea. But for some reason I thought of them during my processing of the choices I had made.

I have always romanticized everything. People, places, events. This drives my husband crazy. He says I always describe people and things better than they really are. I think it all has to do with how I choose to see things.

At a very young age I was made aware of and drawn to the inequities in people's lives. The lives of some people in my community of Roxbury, Massachusetts and those of the white, very wealthy families in Milton, Massachusetts where I attended the prestigious Milton Academy. Boston was a city divided by race but diverse economically within neighborhoods. Blacks lived in certain areas and whites lived in others. City dwelling middle class black families like my own lived in neighborhoods rich with culture and a mixture of income bases. In all of Boston neighborhoods there where grand old Victorian homes, low-income apartment complexes, and public housing. I had a friend in my neighborhood who was very poor and lived in a three-bedroom apartment with her mother, sister and three brothers and a lot of mice and roaches. They would often eat bread sandwiches for breakfast lunch and dinner. Her family was my first experience as a child witnessing people living in severe poverty. I would then travel to Milton and visit homes with indoor swimming pools; horse stables and pets that lived in quarters better than the housing some families in my community lived in. These childhood experiences simmered inside of me for years unchecked. From a very young age I remember experiencing what I would continue to experience throughout my lifetime, a feeling of sitting on the outside looking in as if watching a movie. Staying in the present moment is a modern day mantra encouraged by spiritualists in a quest to stay connected to what we are actually doing in our lives, instead of being led by our thoughts that come and go. But for me, I always seem to be stuck in the present moment, obsessed with observation of people and their actions. I am always so fully absorbed in the energy of a present moment and the need to fulfill the immediate needs of that moment.

Overly sensitive, overly incensed, overly devoted, overly opinionated, overly anxious, overly defensive and overly optimistic, I tried to express this to the judges of the Massachusetts Supreme Judicial Court in my pro se letter written from my prison bunk, in defense of my license to practice law. I wrote to the Honorable Chief Justice and the Justices of the Supreme Judicial Court with all the passion and sensibility that I felt sitting on my prison bunk with no access to Massachusetts' or any other relevant case law to help me defend myself and my license. I wanted to stand before the justices and plead with them to hear and see me. I yearned to convince them that I could still be a good and ethical lawyer and had come so far and learned so much from my experiences that made me, even as a convicted felon, sitting here on this prison bunk, a good and ethical lawyer.

I was serving a 24-month prison sentence at the women's federal prison in Danbury, Connecticut. I plead guilty to the crimes of mail and wire fraud. I abused my power as a lawyer and failed to uphold ethical responsibilities. I confessed this openly and fully, apologizing for my actions and expressing my deep regret.

I tried to humanize myself in their eyes telling them that I was a 45-year old African American woman. I told them I was a wife and mother of three children, ages 26 years old, 13 years old and 8 months old. I wrote that my children were the fourth generation of my family to reside in our home in Roxbury, Massachusetts where members of my family have been leaders and advocates on behalf of our community. My grandmother, Corinne Alleyne, broke the color barrier becoming one of the first black registered public health nurses to practice in a Boston hospital, after having done nursing for many years prior. My parents, Matthew and Dr. Dolores Goode, work tirelessly advocating on behalf of the advancement of people of African Diasporas from Roxbury to New Orleans, Africa, Cuba and the Caribbean. My aunt,

Dr. Delores Gordon-Alleyne, served as the first African American lead pediatrician for Los Angeles County; and I had the honor of being sworn in as a member of the Massachusetts Bar by my uncle, attorney and law professor, Reginald H. Alleyne. My behavior did not reflect the legacy of honesty and integrity taught to me by my family, even though my behavior was driven by that same legacy of love and fight for my people. I explained that I, however, embraced this crisis, as a major catalyst for my personal healing and transformation. I asked the judges to consider my whole person, life and professional experiences, in determining my ability to continue as a lawyer.

In his book, *The Soul of the Law,* Benjamin Sells, a psychotherapist and lawyer who specializes in counseling legal professionals, captures the impact of the debilitating consequences that flow from the abstraction of law and lawyers. He indicates that the very things that the law tries to avoid in its abstract struggle with everyday life are what return in its own life, just as repressed passion can come back as incivility and repressed emotion as ethical breakdown. [x]

In *The Spiritualization of the Legal Profession*, David Hall, former dean and law professor at Northeastern University School of Law, states that

this abstraction and separation can create serious psychological and spiritual discord for some lawyers because some of the abstract mandates of law are in conflict with some of the personal desires and emotional vulnerabilities of the person... Thus there exists unresolved tension and dynamics between law and caretakers of the legal system that can become dysfunctional.[xi] *Some of our waters are troubled because they were troubled long before we ever became lawyers and nothing in the process of our education or work provided any new paths to healing.*[xii] *Ethics like love, emerges from a source within human beings that is deeper than the mind... A true ethical commitment to anything comes from the heart and soul of the person. The mental mastery of the rules is like the stones on the riverbed... It gives shape and contour to the river and provides some limits and protection, but it does not provide the true internal power and energy needed to master this aspect of life and lawyering... Unless the lawyer understands and stays in touch with her soul, then her ethical commitment is superficial and vulnerable... When you see ethical responsibility as an external power that imposes sanctions for improper behavior, then it leaves a gaping hole for abuses and violations... If the external power is all we focus on, then a keen analytical mind will be encouraged to find ways to circumvent or rationalize away that power. As difficult as it is to obtain, we must discover ways to nurture and cultivate the souls of lawyers so that their ethical responsibility is coming from a deeper and more meaningful place... It must come from a place that creates some support and understanding when challenging the tempting situations that arise. Lawyers must develop a perspective about ethics and tempting situations that permits them to see and understand what is internally and spiritually at risk.*[xiii]

I cited my former law school dean in such great detail, as his book was the only research source I had available to me in the prison to try and defend my law license, as well as the only thing I felt that spoke to my aberrant behavior.

Many of my problems were caused by a culmination of obstacles, losses and disappointments that left me with feelings of fear, anger, sadness and alienation. Increasingly I failed to handle strong emotions well. Already physically and emotionally exhausted I embarked on a solo practice in a resource deprived section of Roxbury, plagued by poverty, homicide, joblessness, predatory lending and homelessness. My clients were banks and mortgage companies for whom I handled residential real estate closings. With little to no oversight I received all closing documents and instructions via email or fax and administered millions of dollars in closing money. The terms of the loans were predatory and often not what was promised by the lenders prior to the borrowers coming to the closing table. I internalized these and other struggles of the people in the community with an attitude of defiance toward the lenders that culminated in a state of egotistical anarchy. I buried myself in one community dilemma after another while continuing to hide from my own internal discord, creating destructive and harmful habits while using the excuse of helping the community as a justification for my own wrong behavior. Using the lenders' money gave me power. External, superficial and hollow power and I lost my way. Buddhist monk Thic Nhat Hanh teaches that taking refuge in our work on social justice will cause us to suffer if we continue to ignore our unhappiness and delude ourselves into thinking that we create escape. He states that we can't work for the well-being of others and realize social change when we cannot touch the seeds of our own unhappiness.

I wrote and wrote to the judges and poured out everything I could think of to say to demonstrate a more complete account of my life and character as a private citizen, and a lawyer. I did not want to lose my ticket, or get my ticket punched, as the old timers referred to disbarment. I reflected deeply about my reasons for selecting law as my profession. I explained that I remained passionate about the work of zealous representation on behalf of disadvantaged populations and that I now understood the professional and personal complexities of this work. It is not a battle to be hard fought and won at all costs. Instead, it is a calling that requires emotional intelligence and awareness, not of our limits and boundaries, but of our infiniteness and the courage to choose to live life truly believing that by just being the change myself, I can change the world.

I got disbarred. I read the decision during mail call in the crowded, noisy prison hallway. Gulping back tears I folded the letter from the Massachusetts Supreme Judicial Court back into its envelope and folded that into another envelope and mailed it home to my husband. As crushed as I felt at that moment, it was also strangely liberating for me. Finally, after my personal and professional struggles and coming to federal prison, I was free to start over and just be me.

LOSING OUR MICROWAVES

Easter was cooking us a lot of stuff for the Saturday night movie. Whenever you plan to cook you have to reserve microwave time. That was my job, seeing that I hadn't mastered the art of organizing a meal in prison, acquiring all of the necessary ingredients, and then cooking them in a microwave oven. We're talking everything from fried rice, potato logs, caramel popcorn, peanut butter stew, nachos, salmon cakes, and everything and anything that you can imagine can be made with mackerel. The cheesecakes weren't bad either.

The only time we got to eat a meal that resembled anything close to tasty was when someone prepared it in one of the microwaves available to us for cooking food purchased at the commissary. The food we were fed in the dining hall was a catch as catch can of expired, sodium laden, fat filled, processed stuff that the cooks, like Easter, 'Aunt' June, and Brown, managed to work into something edible for the women. All the cooks would somehow, everyday, open the boxes labeled Desert Storm or stamped with expiration dates that were from years passed, and coax the contents of those cans and boxes into three 5,000 calorie meals a day, everyday. Those who could would buy the microwavable commissary food items and add to them some tomatoes, onions and green peppers that would mysteriously appear from the kitchen from time to time, and they would create full course meals.

The microwave pros were always the ones to come up with the contraband vegetables. We didn't have access to fresh vegetables but there was always someone with a side hustle of selling them and other things. You had to be quick about it when cooking in the microwave a contraband green pepper or onion or something else aromatic. Again, timing was everything. One of the prison case managers was known for shaking the place down whenever she smelled onions cooking. Getting caught cooking with contraband vegetables from the kitchen meant some kind of punishment ranging from being put in segregated housing to scooping up goose poop outside, depending on the mood of the officer on duty.

My other job in preparation for Saturday movie night was to reserve the chairs in the T.V. room. Chairs were hard to come by in the T.V. room. There weren't enough for everyone to watch television at the same time. During the weekends our T.V. room was used as the visiting room. Visits ended at 3:00p.m. and we would line up outside of the T.V./ visiting room doors waiting for the officer to give us permission to go in and grab chairs. People would show up early for a place in the chair line toting bags of crotchet and knitting projects, drink coolers, snacks and extra clothing. Everything you would take in a travel bag if you were going on a road trip. As soon as the officer re-opened the room it was a mad dash to find a stack of chairs, pull enough off the pile for your group, and then manage to set them up where you could see the movie.

Once you secured seating in the T.V. room, you settled in and held down your chairs and territory. T.V. room chairs and seating plans were serious business. People even inherited chairs in prime seating areas. As you and your group became regulars in the T.V. room you would eventually establish an area as "yours" and once your seats were set up nobody would bother them because they knew it was "your area" and "your seats". Needless to say, this was a recipe for recurring problems and town hall meetings where the camp administration would lock us out of the T.V. room until we learned to stop bad chair behavior. The lockout never lasted long because by the time the 4:00pm to midnight officer came on he or she would always find a way to justify re-opening the room. More than two hundred women crammed into a hallway with nothing to do and no television was even more unbearable to the officer than listening to the problems about who didn't get a chair.

Getting microwave time is just the beginning. Don't think you're just going to step in and use the microwave without first learning the ways around it. It's a dance down there and you'd better stay in step. It was like the airport runways with the jumbo jets all lined up for takeoff and the little single engines scooting in and out trying to get a patch of runway. Not to mention everyone is staying on schedule because at anytime the officers could come and take the microwaves ovens away as punishment for something going on there or somewhere else in the world.

Anyway, we were discussing the microwaves. There were two microwaves and one sink located in a common area, in front of C Dorm, for use by over 200 women, so getting microwave time was a big deal. As soon as the 4:00pm count cleared it was a race upstairs to the microwave sign up sheet taped to the officer's office door. The reasonable time slots for preparing dinner were from 4-6 p.m. and usually were filled in by whoever was first in line. Each person can sign her name to one 15-minute time slot. If there's a birthday party or you're trying to prepare a few things, everybody in your group has to get up there together so that you can sign up one after another and block out a chunk of microwave time. And don't learn the hard way, like I did, the importance of bringing your own pen to sign up with. A fatal error that could easily translate into not cooking until 7 or 8 p.m. because no pen means you have to let the people behind you go ahead and sign up while you find a pen. When I made the mistake of dashing to the line without my pen I asked the women behind me if she had a pen and she said, "not for you." There were certain cardinal rules such as if someone gives you something out of the ordinary, you say thank you and keep it moving. You don't ask questions like "where did you get this?" And, when you're second in line for the microwave and the rookie in front of you doesn't have a pen, you don't offer them yours. A gesture like that could mean you're not eating until midnight. The Saturday night movie started at 6.

The regulars down there always let me get in real quick to cook my instant rice or noodle soup. That was all I knew how to cook, hence my above- mentioned jobs of microwave signer upper and seat getter. When the pros took something out of the microwave to stir or add more ingredients to, someone would let me jump in quickly and heat up. I forgot to mention that in order to cook you had to own some cooking bowls. You had to buy these from the commissary, but they stopped selling the good ones, large enough to cook something in. Otherwise, like the chairs, you had to wait to have one passed down to you. The things of least value on the street are most valuable in prison. A good-sized plastic bowl is one of those things. I inherited mine from Easter. I retired it to the top shelf of my locker only to be taken out whenever someone said those glorious words to me, "Get your bowl" meaning that somebody cooked and you're getting something good to eat.

The only bowls you could purchase from the commissary were plastic bowls. Just prior to going to prison I worked as a radio producer and host of the morning show on TOUCH 106.1 fm radio in Boston. Of course, I just happened to have reported on a story on toxins in plastic and metal food containers and how traces of the toxin Bisphenol A (BPA) leaked from plastic containers, especially when subject to heat. BPA is a key building block in polycarbonate plastic containers. Numerous studies indicate exposure to low levels of BPA causes a range of serious health effects in laboratory animals. A recent study from the Centers for Disease Control tested a demographically diverse group of almost 400 Americans for evidence of exposure to BPA and found that ninety five percent of study participants had the chemical in their urine.[xiv] BPA has been linked to a variety of health outcomes, which are increasing in the United States and responsible for a major toll on our collective health. These include breast and prostate cancer, and infertility.[xv] An analysis of CDC's data on women's exposures to BPA shows: ninety percent of all women are exposed to BPA at levels within a factor of ten or less from doses shown to increase breast cancer risk and cause permanent changes in genital tract formation. Scientists are debating the appropriate effective dose of BPA from the particular studies that measured these toxic effects.

We constantly cooked and ate out of plastic bowls and any other plastic object that could be transformed into a cooking utensil such as new garbage bags, recycled potato chip bags, instant rice and chicken pouches or any other bag we could find. Even when eating in the dining hall everything was plastic. The trays they fed us on and our cups and utensils. How many times I sat psyching myself up to take the first bite that I again cursed myself for wanting to be such a damn know-it-all. Reading and researching everything all the damn time.

Just when I finally learned how to make a decent peanut butter stew, at least decent enough for me and my prison sister, Monique, (Mo), to get excited about. Just as a sidebar, Mo couldn't cook either. I never told her so, but it's true. She may read this. She knows she's my sister and I love her, but she can't cook. Just before leaving prison after serving seventeen years, Easter sat us down and tried to get us to understand that if we didn't learn something quick, we were going to starve to death once she was gone. By the time I left, Mo and I were down to contraband apples, commissary almonds and occasionally some of 'Aunt' June's chocolate chip cookies. My advice is when you set out to try and create your prison family, always have a back up for everyone with a critical role such as the family cook. Anyway, just as Sister Rama finally got me to learn how to cook down the peanut butter just so, the administration removed all the microwaves. Another change in policy. No more microwaves. And like everything else taken away, no problem. What was once the iron and ironing board soon became our new George Foreman grill. It is what it is, ladies. Pass the potato log.

PRISON CONDITIONS

They say that if you have to go to federal prison you want to be designated to a prison camp. That's the lowest level of security in the federal system. I was feeling grateful that I was up the hill at the camp. The higher security prison down the hill where I went through receiving looked worse. Having said that, the camp was a real shit hole. There was a rumor that the building housed the defendants during Watergate and I was pretty sure that it was the last time any renovations had been made. It was clear that it was not built to house the over 200 women that were crammed in there.

I was warehoused in an old prison. The building was an un-insulated modular type of structure. The bunk beds were old and the mattresses were stained and filthy. The bathrooms were dirty. Not any fault of the incarcerated women whose job it was to clean them, but the bathrooms were so old and overused that even when they had just been cleaned, they were dirty. Emanating body odors were a mainstay.

The living conditions were subhuman. The camp administrator would tell us that our prison wasn't as bad as others so we should be happy. Having been a criminal defense lawyer for many years and visited many prisons I was acutely aware of how bad conditions in general were in many other prisons. The administrator's statement reminded me of the reasoning given by legislators advocating to build new prisons. After ignoring horrendous prison conditions for years, they would suddenly use these inhumane conditions to advocate for the building of newer prisons. But most often this still didn't translate into closing down the older prison once the new one was completed.

Over the years the prison and the prison camp at Danbury have been flipped flopped back and forth from housing men to women. The wear and tear of the building was evident as one that had housed the Watergate men, Reverend Sun Yong Moon, Leona Helmsley and hundreds of thousands of everyday people that came through its doors. The prison camp consisted of one building and an outside recreation area. Our entire existence took place in that building and up and down that one hallway. Two hundred fourteen women crammed side by side in bunks piled on top of each other. One hundred fifty of the women lived in the basement of the building referred to as the dorms. There was A, B, and C Dorm. Each dorm was a room divided up into fifty, two-bunk cubicles. The cubicles were the length of the bunk bed. They had no doors and top bunkers had a bird's eye view of the entire room. There was no privacy. The camp counselor would remind us of this. "You're in prison, you have no privacy," she would tell us. Male officers walked freely in and out of the dorms and bathrooms unannounced, along with the occasional tour group. Sewage and other pipes ran directly over the top bunks where we often returned to our cubicles to find our beds wet from unknown dripping matter. Along with the pipes were electrical wiring and a hodgepodge of tangled wires that were coated with dirt and grime from years of poor ventilation and no upkeep.

Bathrooms separated the dorms between A, B and C dorms. The bathrooms had no ventilation and no windows. The toilets rarely flushed, as the water pressure most days was non-existent due to the inadequacy of the septic system that struggled to keep up with the demand of over 200 women. The smell of fecal matter and other bodily odors were a constant presence in the air.

Like the bathrooms, there was no ventilation system within the dorms. One side of the dorm was windowless and cave-like, as it was on the building side beneath the upstairs hallway. The other side had a row of windows that only partially opened. There was no ventilation. There was no insulation. It was blisteringly hot in the summer and freezing in the winter. The roof leaked and water flooded into the dorms during heavy rain or snow. The same blankets that were given to us for sleeping were used to clean up the floods and leaks of all kinds, including overflowing toilets.

Upstairs from the dorms was a hallway with rooms off of it that housed the rest of the camp population, the administrative offices and the education department. We would often joke that we lived in a hallway, except it wasn't a joke. Absolutely everything we did was in or off of that hallway. And there are women there right now whose lives revolve around that one hallway. Day after day, month after month, year after year, never being able to go beyond that area. The saddest part about it was that the over 1400 women warehoused down the hill in the higher security prison behind the fence looked up at us walking around the building and envied the freedom we had.

One day, on the hallway bulletin board, the administration posted a request for public comment based on an upcoming inspection to be performed by the American Correctional Association. The Commission on Accreditation for Corrections and the American Correctional Association are private, non-profit organizations that direct the accreditation of correctional programs in the United States and other countries. They are bodies comprised of corrections professionals with a responsibility to verify that its over 20,000 membership agencies (prisons), applying for accreditation, comply with the applicable standards. They create the ACA standards which, as described on their website, are the national benchmark for the effective operation of correctional systems throughout the United States and are necessary to ensure that correctional facilities are operated professionally. Agencies (prisons) apply for this accreditation (1) to ensure that the operation is in compliance with national standards, (2) to demonstrate to interested parties that the organization is operating at acceptable professional levels and (3) to comply with court orders.

The ACA is probably most well known for its controversial accreditation program. As the Boston Globe summarized in June 20, 2001: To prison chiefs and jail sheriffs nationwide, it is considered the Good Housekeeping seal of approval for corrections… But a closer look at the accreditation program of the American Correctional Association… shows that it has routinely accredited facilities beset by charges of abuse or poor conditions.[xvi] ACA has an annual tradeshow, dubbed the 'Congress of Corrections', which brings thousands of companies wishing to make a profit off of any sort of incarceration together with thousands of corrections professionals with purchasing power for their facilities. By selling booth space on their convention floor, the ACA pays for its annual convention, and representatives of these companies play a key role in developing the policies which corrections officials use to govern themselves.[xvii]

The prison administration posted, in the hallway, the ACA's request for public comment. The notice instructed the reader as to where to send information relevant to the prison's compliance with the standards at least ten working days prior to the Danbury audit scheduled for March 1. The notice was posted in January. This was no spot check. Once that announcement went up we were ordered by the camp staff into full cleaning and repairing mode. Everything in sight was scrubbed, mowed, painted and steam washed. Still, whatever the reason for Danbury to seek accreditation, the standards had to be extremely low.

Because the notice for comment referred to compliance with standards, I thought it was necessary for us to know what those standards were. How else were we to know if something was below the standard? So I asked the camp administrator for a copy of the ACA standards. His initial response to me was that the basic standards were the basis for the Federal Bureau of Prisons program statements and that I could find them by looking up those program statements. Now, there were hundreds of Bureau of Prisons program statements covering everything from staff hiring to how to place food orders. Even if I could sit somewhere and hunt through the maze of hundreds of program statements there was nothing to identify which of them specifically was applicable for an ACA accreditation audit. A week later I went back to him and stated that I was unable to make an informed and appropriate response to the request for public comment without knowledge of the basic standards specific to an accreditation audit. He told me he would provide them to me.

As of February 8th I still had not received the standards and, with time being of the essence, I went back to request them again. This time the camp administrator told me he was not going to give them to me. He said that they were going through their most important audit and he said, "Do you think I am going to give them to some inmate so that you can pick through them and find every little discrepancy." I forgot to mention that this all started mainly because I had been asking for more than a year for hand soap to be provided in the bathrooms. They provided sanitary napkins but no soap. I wanted soap in the bathrooms and I was hoping the basic standards could help me get it.

Finally, the administrator told me he decided not to give me a copy of the standards but he would allow me to look through the standards in his office. I arrived at his office at the scheduled time and by then he had decided not to let me look through the standards myself but that he wanted to know specifically what I wanted information about and he would look it up and read the standard to me, also cautioning me that he didn't have a lot of time to do this. I decided to ask if there was a standard for providing hand soap in bathrooms. He held the book up and read something to me that was remotely related to cleaning supplies and then told me. “No. There’s no standard that requires us to provide inmates (he loved that label. We were “these inmates”, “these fucking inmates”, “our inmates”) with hand soap in the bathrooms.” He then said, “How about this? Every time an inmate comes out of the bathroom, I’ll have an officer standing wearing a soap dispenser on his belt and he can shoot some to the inmate to wash her hands with.” I wasn’t sure how to respond or if he were serious. After all, I had attended many town hall meetings in the hallway when he very seriously had come up with other ‘solutions’ that were just as kooky. As a side bar, many of us formerly incarcerated people are encouraging the end of the use of the term inmate and replacing it with the term incarcerated or formerly incarcerated people.

From January to March, in preparation of the ACA inspection, the women were ordered and occasionally put on lock down, to make us get the prison ready. The inspection day came and went. Period. The inspectors made a brisk pass through of the prison camp and were gone. We were later thanked for helping Danbury to pass inspection and offered ice cream. Still we had no hand soap in the bathrooms.

A MOTHER'S LOVE

The pain is overflowing in the women.
Ever brimming, spilling over the edge.
At moments, in the classroom. On our bunks.
Cleaning toilets. Mowing lawns.
Our heavy hearts overflow. Sagging.
A child leaves the visiting room pleading with his mother.
How much longer? How much longer?
The love of a mother fills up sagging like the magnolias
heavy, waiting for their love to be carried further.

Many incarcerated women have children. The women are in prison, but still are mothers who love their children deeply. They do their best to mother from prison. Standing at the crowded telephones trying myself to still be a wife and mother, I often heard many conversations about things going on with the children of the women in Danbury. While talking to your children from a telephone in prison, every conversation is a clipped verbal dance of concern, love, anger, discipline and inquisition. Missed weddings, anniversaries, graduations and funerals. A young boy's hamster died. A daughter's details of abuse in the hands of her caregivers. Requests for pictures for lockers full of childhood histories over the years, as they've grown while their mothers were warehoused in a prison.

For women in prison, every request made to the outside regarding the care of their children is a cause for caution and concern. Fear of signing the wrong paper that could result in someone taking their children away. It often causes a paralysis in the women as to how to make decisions regarding requests for things such as the signing of power of attorneys and temporary guardianships. Fear of doing something that could be construed as giving away their parental rights.

The Rebecca Project for Human Rights reports, twenty-five years ago, the presence of women – especially mothers- was an aberration in the criminal justice system. That was before the war on drugs. Since 1986, following the introduction of mandatory sentencing to the federal drug laws in the mid 1980's, and its adoption by many states at about the same time, the number of women in prison has risen 400 percent, according to a recent Department of Justice report, *Survey of State Prison Inmates*. For black women, the figure is 800 percent.[xviii]

The result is the United States now incarcerates more than 215,000 women and nearly two-thirds of these women are African American or Latina, and more than ninety percent have been convicted of nonviolent offenses.[xix] They exist mostly as caricatures of the ultimate bad mother. They are viewed as mothers who violated the basic maternal commitment to care for their children and instead engaged in wrongful criminal activities…but in truth, mothers' pathways to incarceration are complex, and most often rooted in issues of sexual and physical violence.[xx] The reality is, seventy-some percent of our female population are low-level, non-violent offenders. The fact that they have even come into prison is a question mark for me… Most of these women would have gotten probation years ago.[xxi]

The women were in prison for all kinds of things, mostly related to money or drugs. But none of what most did warranted the lengths of sentences and the effects on their families. When women are in prison their families suffer. A woman I met in Danbury had already been there for four of the eight years she was sentenced to for selling heroin. One day, just before Thanksgiving, she sat down next to me and picked up a conversation we had a few weeks earlier about her 15-year old daughter being sexually active.

"Can you believe it?" She said. "Now my other daughter

is using drugs and they want me to sit here for another four years. I can't do nothing to help my kids and my son now thinks God is a liar because I keep telling him to have faith that I will be able to come home, but he doesn't believe it anymore. He says he doesn't believe in God anymore either. We got nothing to do here". She said. "We just sit around here doing nothing. I sat here for four years doing nothing and they want me to sit for another four. For what? I can't do nothing to help my kids. What's the good in that?"

The role that mothers play as parents during their incarceration is minimal as a result of the nature of the correctional system. Given these constraints, it is not surprising that mothers express feelings of inadequacy, despondency, and fear of permanent loss of their children. Furthermore because their own behavior has caused the separation, most mothers feel intense guilt and shame.[xxii]

Mother's Day 2010 in Danbury was a day heavy with the emotions of women missing their families. Among the women that received a visit that day was a woman who came to prison when her son was only three years old. He was now sixteen years old and came to see her for Mother's Day, alone, for the first time. Another young mother who had just started serving a 10-year mandatory minimum sentence for selling drugs was visited by her four sons, ages 14, 10, 6, and 17 months. This was their first time seeing her since her incarceration. They were brought to the prison from Washington D.C. by an organization called Our Place that brings children to visit their mothers in prison. Later that day the woman sat on the stairs outside of the visiting room weeping because her 17 month old baby boy wouldn't come to her during the visit. He cried the entire time. A father came to visit his daughter but was turned away because he did not know that it wasn't her designated visiting day. It was Mother's Day, but you could only get a visit if it was your visiting day. Like all other weekends, some women got visits, most didn't. And some would remember this Mother's Day more than others.

The New York Daily News headline read, MOM'S DAY HORROR: 2 Teens killed, Woman Wounded After Gunman Taunts Mother at Bronx Party. The article read,

Mother's Day dawned tragically in the Bronx when two innocent teenagers were killed at a party when they tried to defend a friend's mom, police said yesterday.

Quanisha Wright, 16 was shot along with Marvin Wiggins Jr., 15, after she stood up for their friend's mother in the face of a gunman's taunts, witnesses said.

Quanisha Wright, who had just celebrated her sweet 16 birthday on Friday, was shot at a party for a 1 year old on Weeks Ave. in the Bronx.

"How could they take my little girl away over nothing?" Asked her heartbroken dad, John Barnwell. "She was the sweetest girl. She never hurt a soul."

Quanisha, a student at the Bronx Leadership Academy, was raised by her grandmother because her mother, Desseray Wright, is in prison.[xxiii]

Every now and then Desseray would pull out the photo book and we would look at the pictures of Quanisha. A beautiful girl with two braids framing her smiling face. Some days if you just looked at Desseray too long she would be overwhelmed with sadness.

There was no special consideration provided to Desseray by the Federal Bureau of Prisons after her daughter's death except that she was finally, after five years of being warehoused in a federal prisons across the country, allowed to be transferred to Danbury, Connecticut where I met her, so that now she could be closer to her remaining two sons living in the Bronx.

Desseray was incarcerated for selling drugs and was serving a ten-year mandatory minimum sentence. Although at the time of Quanisha's death Des had served more than half of her sentence and had two teenage sons living with their grandmother in the Bronx, New York, all of whom were struggling even more now with the loss of Quanisha, it was still deemed necessary to continue warehousing Desseray in a low-level prison camp in Danbury, Connecticut, just a few miles from her home and children.

The Federal Bureau of Prisons has at its discretion compassionate release, but to date it has only rarely been used to release prisoners who are terminally ill and in their final days. There is no greater retribution than the loss of a child such as Quanisha Wright. Desseray had served more than half of her drug sentence, participated in rehabilitative programs as well as worked for Unicor. She was designated to the lowest security level within the federal prison system where the women drove vehicles, moved freely on the prison grounds and went outside the grounds to help clean the town of Danbury and speak to high school students about staying out of trouble. Yet, Des still could not go home to rebuild the lives of her remaining children instead of being warehoused in a prison. Eating and sleeping day in and day out, while working at Unicor and being paid a few cents per hour.

Not too long after Desseray's daughter's death, Nancy Flores was grieving her 17-year old son's death. He had been shot multiple times. On the day Nancy and her sister Maricelis had been informed of his death their screams and wails brought the prison to a standstill. At the time we didn't know what happened but we knew from the appearance of the chaplain and the moaning of the women, that a family member had probably died.

I had come to know Nancy because her younger sister Maricelis was a student in the English as a second language class I taught. Nancy spoke even less English than Maricelis, but would stop me in the hallway everyday to ask whether her youngest sister was paying attention in class. Maricelis had arrived at Danbury with a 60-month sentence for selling crack cocaine. She was a young, 24-year old mother from Puerto Rico. Her way of communicating to everyone was a smile. As co-defendants in the same drug case, Maricelis, Nancy and six other of their brothers and sisters and three nieces and nephews were sentenced and dispersed from Puerto Rico to federal prisons throughout the country. Their elderly parents were left to care for all of the very young children of these siblings and were now dealing with the death of Nancy's son and trying to raise money for a funeral.

As a family their troubles had been on going for sometime. I gave a writing assignment in class one day and with the help of her English-Spanish dictionary Maricelis wrote about her struggles and a life of "a lot of sadness and pain." She was married at 15, divorced after two years and started using and selling drugs. At age 16 her niece was gunned down in front of her and soon after that she gave birth to her daughter. Three weeks later, her daughter's father was murdered. Maricelis described this time as so traumatic that she thought of killing herself but didn't want to leave her daughter. Years after her involvement in drug selling had ended, she, with most of her other siblings and many other family members, was prosecuted and sentenced to federal prison for 5 or more years. She described this as something that destroyed her family but that God gave her the strength to keep moving.

Desseray was working down in the kitchen when she heard that Nancy's son had been killed and she went up to the chapel to console her. Des said that she just wanted to give Nancy support because she knew what the woman was feeling. We often experienced times when both Nancy and Des would be inconsolable as they continued to mourn for their children.

During my incarceration, I was deeply affected by the great number of women that would remain there long after I had left. Most of these women were serving very long federal mandatory minimum or guideline sentences for participation in drug selling. Most of them were mothers. Their sentences were unreasonably long, the average being ten years. They had been in prison long after what should have been considered fair sentences. The women were provided very limited educational and employment training opportunities. Yet they managed to hold it together while psychologically dealing with enduring such long sentences. They remained positive and hopeful amidst a torrent of regret, heartache, remorse, alienation, loneliness, and a host of other problems, mostly related to being in prison while their children struggled to survive. Prison is the place where statistics come to life.

There are currently more than two million children in this country with one or both parents incarcerated. Most of these incarcerated parents are first time, nonviolent offenders serving drug related sentences. A large number of them have not seen their children since they were incarcerated because many families are unable to visit due to the lack of resources to travel long distances to far away prisons. 62 percent of parents in state prisons and 84 percent of parents in federal prison are held over 100 miles from their last residence. In federal prisons, about 43 percent of parents are held over 500 miles from their homes.

Often multiple family members are incarcerated simultaneously for the same drug offense. Desseray Wright for example is the cousin and co-defendant of my friend at Danbury, Monique Williams, who is also serving a ten-year mandatory minimum drug sentence. Like Des, Monique is a mother of two children and her husband is also incarcerated for the same drug case. There were many others with multiple members of the same family in prison. Their children are among the over two million children with one or both parents incarcerated.

The effect of a mother's arrest and incarceration on a family is often more disruptive than that of a father's arrest and incarceration.[xxiv] That is because approximately two-thirds of incarcerated mothers are the primary caregivers for at least one child before they were arrested.[xxv] In contrast, only half of incarcerated fathers were living with their youngest child prior to incarceration.[xxvi]

When I came to prison my son was 6 months old. During those early visits he didn't remember me. He cried and clung to my husband when I would try to hold him. I had to remind myself that I was very fortunate. My husband brought my children to see me every weekend. There were many women who hadn't seen their children and wouldn't see them for a very long time. Many women leave prison after being incarcerated for years and do not know where their children are. Some states relinquish rights of a parent if the parent is "out of the child's life" for more than two years and under the federal Adoption and Safe Families Act of 1997, parental rights can be terminated if a child as been in foster care 15 of the last 22 months.[xxvii] Some of this "absence" is a result of the complexity of navigating the logistics of arranging visitation to correctional facilities.

According to the Vera Institute of Justice, once case workers learn of parental incarcerations, they must navigate the corrections system as secure facilities, jails, and prisons have elaborate and time-consuming procedures regarding visits to prisoners. Corrections officials must receive prior notification of a visit to insure the parent's presence in the visiting room, and caseworkers need to prepare children for what they will experience when entering a jail or prison. Finally, caseworkers need to schedule transportation, and either a caseworker or other staff member must accompany foster children during these visits. In sum, arranging visits to prisons is not a task easily under taken by individual caseworkers.[xxviii]

Because so many women upon leaving prison are homeless with no money or access to resources, reuniting with their families becomes all that more difficult. One woman described to me her experience as "I've been locked up for twelve years. They kept me in prison and stupid and now they tell me its time for me to get out, find a job with no skills, find a place to live that I can afford. Find food and clothing, and I'm leaving here with nothing. I can't even remember how to pay a bill. The system didn't require me to do anything but stay in prison." Discharged women prisoners with drug convictions who mange to reunite with their children face another set of challenges. Because they have been convicted of drug crimes, they are subject to federal bans on public housing, welfare and other social services.[xxix]

In addition to the many barriers to maintaining family ties, overcrowded conditions were also problematic for our visitors at the Danbury prison camp. Our television room/chapel/occasional classroom became our weekend visiting room. But, of course, when it came to the prison administration providing adequate space for visitors, overcrowding wasn't the problem. The problem was the visitors. Because of the limited space at the camp, the visiting policy kept changing. The last change was from an even/odd system to an accumulated point system. The camp administrator told us that we needed to get together and make sure that everyone was able to get a visit and that the "problem" was the family members that came on every available visiting day and took up space in the visiting room. That was the problem. Husbands, children, mothers and fathers coming to visit their mothers, wives, sisters and daughters. Taking advantage of every opportunity they could to see their loved one. That was the problem, not that the prison crammed over two hundred women in a space built to accommodate less than a third of that number and that there was no place adequate for families of those women to visit. Visitors were the problem and if we didn't make it work the response would be to regulate visits even more. Without visitation, the government imposes a double punishment on convicted parents: in addition to loss of liberty, lack of contact may further strain parent-child relationships. In the worst case, lengthy separation without visits leads to the permanent dissolution of the family.[xxx]

Another devastating impact of the separation of parent and child due to incarceration of one or both parents is the feelings of isolation, fear, shame and guilt often experienced by the children left behind. The Osborne Association found that children of incarcerated parents are more likely to experience fear, anxiety, sadness, loneliness, and guilt. Their self-esteem was lower; they were more likely to be depressed, and to withdraw from remaining family and friends. This leads to greater likelihood of problems at school, as well as other antisocial behaviors.[xxxi] According to the Women's Prison and Home Association, Inc., children of offenders are five times more likely than their peers to end up in prison themselves. One in 10 will be incarcerated before reaching adulthood.[xxxii] According to the Child Welfare League of America, it was projected that approximately fifty percent of the children of incarcerated parents will enter the juvenile justice system before their eighteenth birthday. While I was in Danbury the New Britain Herald Newspaper reported in February of 2010 that in Connecticut seventy percent of juvenile detainees had parents who were incarcerated, according to the state's court support services division.

Something I never thought about prior to going to prison in relation to women and mandatory minimum sentences was that the very nature of mandatory minimums, their lengthy time spans, often takes from women their child bearing years. Mandatory minimum sentences do much more than just put individuals in prisons. When we link harsh, lengthy sentences to the waste of human potential it also encompasses the ability to start a family.

Prison allowed me to see the spirit of a woman in all women, through all the heavy labels, bad mother, inmate, convict, felon, junkie, crack whore and thief. The labels exact further external and internal punishment long after incarceration and created further disconnect from families and communities. Sisterhood in a prison broke through that for me, allowing me to feel the real person. It's the one place where the simplest gesture can be a warm lifesaver just at the right time by a person you came to understand and appreciate. I learned the true profile of who is in this county's prisons and how wrong it is to put people in cages unnecessarily. Particularly women with children.

BLANKET WARS

I lay on my bunk and couldn't believe how beautiful the full moon was. I wanted to know why the moon was there and so bright in the night sky? Did the full moon have anything to do with the earlier blanket and sheet shake down? That's when the officers who ran the laundry would go through all the units pulling apart our beds and tearing through our lockers in search of extra blankets or sheets and of course anything else contraband they may have come across.

There is never the issue of probable cause in prison. No procedural due process. No burden on the officers to establish a basis for search and seizure. My strategy for avoiding shakedowns was to keep my locker in as much disarray as I could. Not a huge challenge for me. Although I am a compulsive hand and everything else washer, I am not neat, nor well organized. It took Miss Virginia more than a few lessons with me to teach me how to fold my t-shirts and prison uniforms so that everything would fit in my locker. When you opened my locker door something would fall out. I never used the lock for my locker. I didn't need it. Everyone knew that you just never went into my locker for anything. It was a hazard area. My bunkie at the time, Rhonda, would laugh at me but she was always the one getting shaken down. Her locker was neat. Everything in its place. No excess anything. And she got shaken down every time some cop didn't know what to do with himself during his shift. Me. Never. Except during a laundry shakedown.

During the winter months, which were the longest in Connecticut, the cold and wet would settle in early and we would try our best to find ways to keep dry and warm. I would collect used water bottles and at bedtime I would fill them with hot water and place them under my covers to take the chill off long enough for me to fall asleep. This particular shakedown took place one freezing cold, snowy day in February 2011, one of the coldest winters on record when the snow drifts were past our windows. Melted snow leaked into our living spaces from the roof and under doorways.

The Federal Bureau of Prisons had recently changed a women's prison camp in Pekin, Illinois to a men's facility and they were dispersing the women to prison camps all over the country. The shakedown was in anticipation of Danbury receiving 25 of the Pekin women. My friend, Arlinda Johns, a.k.a Tray, was one of the women transferred from Pekin and she described how the Pekin prison informed them of their transfer and how it was carried out. Tray said *"On Valentine's Day of 2011, a town hall meeting was called and the women at the Pekin camp were informed that the camp would be converted from women to men. We were also told that the Bureau of Prisons would try to place us within our region when designating us to new prisons, those being Waseca, Minnesota or Greenville, Illinois. Around March 10th, 23 names were placed on the call out. We were told to pack out and watch the call out sheet. On March 17th during the 9:30p.m. count we were told to report to the visiting room. We were loaded on to a bus and about five hours into the ride we were told that we were going to Danbury, Connecticut. One bus change and twenty hours later we arrived in the middle of the night."* Having been only a few hours from her son while at Pekin, Tray was now designated to the prison at Danbury located over 1,000 miles away from her family. So that's why the laundry shakedown. Already over-crowded and short on everything, the race was on at Danbury to search out any extra bed linen. The word went out and everyone scrambled to hide their goods as we saw the officer in charge of laundry descending into the dorms. Although you're allowed two blankets, somehow, of course, both of my blankets were confiscated during the shakedown.

When I told the laundry officer of her mistake, that I had been left with no blankets, she told me that she didn't know what happened to my blankets, that she was done with the shakedown, and she was done with our conversation.

Now you have to understand, not only was it one of the coldest days of the year, I happened to have been sleeping in C-25, the coldest room in the prison. I had asked for months to be moved to this cube even though it was cold, because it had a window that allowed in fresh air and it was the furthest cubicle from the unventilated bathroom. But it was cold. It abutted a door leading outside that was constantly opening and closing in a steady stream of traffic. I was upset about losing my blankets. Mine weren't just any old blankets. I had managed over time to trade up, blanket after blanket to finally have two really good, heavy, blankets with no stains or rips. I had hand washed these blankets and my sheets weekly to avoid losing them to the new laundry policy that no longer allowed us to wash our blankets and sheets with our clothing. Instead, we had to exchange them at designated times for "clean" ones. It was a catch-as-catch can, an 80/20 chance that you would get something you would feel comfortable sleeping on. Eighty percent of the time you wouldn't. Most of the blankets were old and worn and looked like they came out of the trunk of someone's car after being used to change tires and clean up more than a few quarts of oil. These were the same blankets that would be used to mop up overflowing toilets and other large spills. So to get good, clean blankets was truly a treasure and to lose one, never mind two, in a shakedown was a huge set back in the battle to eke out a semblance of quality of life.

The laundry officer dismissed me knowing that I had no blankets on one of the coldest days of the winter. I stewed over this as I gazed up at an amazing moon. I wondered about two things. Whether she appreciated how wonderful her life was. She, and her husband who also worked at the prison, had the freedom to go home everyday and spend time with their family. How amazing that was. When you understand and appreciate that, how could you ever be filled with such indifference for another person? How could you be unkind to anyone when you have the precious freedom of movement and freedom to hold and love your husband and children? When I was incarcerated I remember watching the officers come and go from the prison and I just wanted to go too. Just to be able to leave the confines of the prison and see my family and the outside world again.

What also came to mind as I lay staring at the moon was the fact that we even exist as human beings on this amazing planet spinning around in this vast universe. If it weren't for the gravitational influence of this beautiful moon we would probably not exist because planet earth would not have been stable enough to sustain life. I read somewhere that the moon keeps the earth balanced enough and in just the right position to sustain and grow life. How amazing is that?

If we lived in awareness of how fragile our existence is on this planet we would refocus our energy as a human race to study and discover the most productive ways for us to continue to survive, not as hoarders and usurpers, haves and have-nots, but as resources of the planet. We must learn to commune, understand and relate to the energies and rhythms of the other phenomena that we are connected to that make up this planet on whose very thin outer layer we manage to exist. Our focus should be not on building and sustaining prisons, but healing the people who have been targeted to fill the prisons. What's a blanket between two people who are lucky everyday to even exist?

It was interesting that the officers easily treated us so poorly particularly considering that it was because of us that they had jobs that allowed them to be so self-righteous, condescending and cold, particularly with the state of the economy at that time. Everyday in the news we heard that the unemployment rate was very high. You would think that they would have come to work everyday with open arms and bearing gifts to all of us. Thanking us for being there. After all, instead of us being allowed out to use our labor force to generate revenue to feed and clothe our own children, our revenue had been transferred for the benefit of their households.

By warehousing people in prisons for long periods of time we essentially redirect money and capital flows away from the communities that are disproportionately represented within the prison system, equaling poor communities of color. The money shifts from providing for already mostly poor children to maintaining money flows to continue feeding, clothing and educating mostly children of middle class parents. Many who are former military, as prison jobs have become a partial solution for the surplus labor problem amongst veterans.

I'm sorry to also report that many people are already imprisoned without actually being in prison. We think small. We function in relative unawareness about ourselves and our connection to everything around us. One day a young 20-something year old officer, exasperated with the back talk he was getting from a woman, yelled, "I'm in prison too, in here everyday with you." I suggested to him that now might be a good time for him to walk straight out to his car, drive home, grab a backpack and go hike the Himalayas. His concept of where he "was" encompassed a hallway in the Danbury federal prison. He didn't consider that he was also just feet from the front door that he could freely walk out of. He could get in his car and travel anywhere in the state of Connecticut. He could travel throughout the United States. He could go to infinity and beyond, exploring numerous continents and oceans that are rooted to a planet that is spinning on its axis, while rotating around a sun that is part of the galaxy called the Milky Way, which by the way, is just one of millions of galaxies in the Universe. I think this is how I started this whole chapter, but my point is I'm not sure what he was thinking about as he stood in the hallway screaming about being in prison too. At that moment he was more in prison, for sure, than Annie, the incarcerated woman he was speaking to. Annie subscribed to Sun Magazine. Enough said.

Reaching that place of awareness is different for all of us obviously, if we ever get to it. I think however, it's part of the answer to what else to do with people than warehousing them in prisons. Helping people become more aware. Mostly people are imprisoned by their thoughts, emotions, fears, egos, long before they are physically imprisoned. Where do we get the ideas that shape our daily lives? How do we make a living? How do we come to accept a job where we have to come to work everyday in a place we hate and be mean to people. What shapes our decisions? What's allowable? What should we act like, dress like, look like? Who is worthy of recognition? Who is smart enough? Who deserves food, water and shelter? A good education, sustainable employment, and healthcare? A quality life? Who should be at the table when it comes to making the rules? Who should decide who should be sent to live in a cage and who decided that that will make things better and everybody on the outside safer?

Prison is dehumanizing. It severs the ties of the incarcerated to healthy human interaction and relationships. Most people in prison already struggle with creating healthy relationships, some having never experienced one. The prison culture of cold, impersonal detached treatment of those imprisoned exacerbates and perpetuates this breakdown of relationship building that is crucial to the transformation and healing of people. The Buddhist monk and ex-incarcerated person, Fleet Maul, stated, "It's not just the incarcerated people who are affected by these hellholes, it's the prison staff as well. The rates of alcoholism, child abuse, spousal abuse, and suicide are all off the charts among prison workers." [xxxiii]

In the 18 months I spent at Danbury, I heard of three officers and one incarcerated woman who committed suicide there. Two of the officers shot themselves in the head and the other officer hung himself in staff housing with a cord to an air conditioner. The incarcerated woman was in her 40s and had just started an 11-year sentence. She hung herself in the shower. Besides being locked down for a while and the flag flying at half staff on behalf of one of the officers, nothing was ever disclosed about the deaths, adding to the muted, suffocating impact of the prison environment. My dear Buddhist aunt, Darla Martin, sent me an article by Ruth Dennison, a legendary Vipassana teacher. In it Dennison refers to this as a collective karma, where because people are members of a society they must share in experiencing the consequences.

Our collective wellbeing as human beings is directly impacted by what energy is mass-produced among us. We live in a country where there is a proliferation of prisons and this energy affects all of us far beyond the prison wall. From cheering for the death penalty at a debate for republican candidates for the presidency of the United States, to the executions of potentially innocent people such as Troy Davis, the murdering of our children like Trayvon Martin and so many others, and the dehumanizing practice of locking people in prison cells for unconscionably long periods of time, affects all of us. The madness of our penal policies and the criminal-justice system places the entire society at risk. Dismantling the prison industrial complex represents the great moral assignment and political challenge of our time.[xxxiv]

Most of the people I came in contact with who worked as corrections staff did not communicate with us nicely. I can't speak for how they conducted themselves in their personal lives, but at the prison, overall, they were not kind people. There were some caring officers. A few. Mr. Hewitt, Mr. B, Ms. M, Ms. Longo and Mr. Kinnel were all kind and caring people. They always maintained a level of human kindness. Mr. Kinnel allowed me to sit in the dining hall and write when it wasn't mealtime. Every other kitchen officer, except Ms. M, always sent me and my papers packing. There were no other accessible places in the prison to write. I can't think of any other genuinely and consistently kind officers that I came in contact with. Except maybe the woman who cleaned my teeth and patched the hole in my tooth long enough for me to get out and get it fixed. It was either pull it or live with the pain and I preferred to hold on to my lower front tooth. She didn't actually work for the prison.

Most of the officers were just creepy. I couldn't ever get a sense of how they were able to disconnect from us so easily. There was a culture of small-mindedness that permeated the environment. I couldn't imagine having a job where you chose to be mean. You chose everyday to come to work and instead of finding ways to be positive and uplifting to probably the most needy segment of the world's population, you created and perpetuated a system that was demeaning and mean.

The prison administration harassed us about the most trivial issues such as how to make our beds and to keep our uniform shirts tucked in. All of this was in the guise of prison safety, however major security breaches were always only detected by a mistake on behalf of one of the women doing something crazy. Some of the comments and behavior of prison staff was so off-centered and unbelievable that it was comical. There was, for example, the speech given to us during admission and orientation (A&O). A&O is for new women. You attend it sometime after you arrive. For me I had been there a month before A&O was held. At Danbury A&O is an all day event when the officers from different departments come and tell you what they do and how it affects you as an incarcerated person. The day opens with the camp counselor giving an overview of life in prison. During my A&O we were encouraged to be convicts, not inmates. I remember thinking, are you kidding me? I was still having a tough time identifying as an inmate, and now this? A woman who worked as a cleaner was in the room at the time and the counselor pointed her out and used her as an example of what she meant by convict. "Now you see her over there?" "She's a convict." Said the counselor. The woman shifted awkwardly not sure how to react. The counselor went on to encourage us to be convicts, not inmates. Convicts took it on the chin, sucked it up, accepted the situation, got over it and did what you had to do to get by and didn't complain about it. She continued on. "So what if you get punished for something and I take your phone privileges away for 6 months, you're a convict. So what if you don't have visits for 3 months. You're a convict. Inmates complain all the time and write to everybody including the President. Convicts don't. They just suck it up. Be a convict, not an inmate". Okay I guess my list of things I brought to A&O with me would not be addressed. There were just a few things anyway. A better mattress; a room with a window; and getting some Stevia and fresh vegetables added to the items on commissary.

Former incarcerated person and Buddhist monk, Fleet Maul, stated, "The whole structure of incarceration is shame-based. It is a process by which you are continually forced to die to every aspect of yourself that gives you dignity. Guards are constantly derisive. Regardless of whether you're in prison for tax evasion or murder, the message is the same:

you're subhuman, you don't count".[xxxv] If we got an opportunity to say something to an officer, you had to get everything out of your mouth as quickly as possible because if not you would be talking to their backs as they walked away. When you did get a chance to have a conversation, you usually sounded like a raving, rambling lunatic because once you realized you were actually getting a chance to have their attention, you would get tongue tied trying to get out everything you've wanted to say since the day you walked in the door. The strangeness of it was that while they would stand as far away from you as possible when speaking to you and usually answer you with disdain, while doing so they would often turn and call out to a co-worker with civilities and pleasantries that would now sound like a native language you spoke long ago. I'd hear them talking amongst themselves and I too would want to wave and yell out "hey girl, how was dinner last night?" It's as if the staff have decided that incarcerated people also needed to be denied the status of personhood.

The title inmate became our first name. We had a P.A. system at Danbury that was used by staff to call us. Even the prison psychologist and chaplain would page us using the term inmate. Inmate, inmate, inmate. We would hear that screamed over the P.A. system all day, everyday. Ironically earlier in the same week that I became aware that both the psychologist and the chaplain also addressed us as inmate, I was reading a book by Buddhist monk, Thich Nhat Hanh, and Jesuit priest, Daniel Berrigan. In it Berrigan states that it's intolerable for a priest to have the same keys that the guards and the warden have so that he comes and goes freely… It seems to me if one is going to be chaplain, he should say, 'I won't keep a single key'… He needs the essential modesty of a prisoner. Then he could test his own formulas of faith, which he's asking the prisoner to believe.[xxxvi]

My prison experience changed me. I find myself listening to people as they talk and looking for signs of bullshit or meanness. I look at people and wonder if they have the ability, if put in the right environment, to allow people to persuade them to treat others like they are less than human or unworthy of kindness and compassion. This is a bad way to treat people. Crime is a result of a breakdown or spiritual disconnect long before the offender winds up in a prison and a lot of crime, such as drug addiction, is not crime at all, but a public health issue. The further dehumanizing culture of prison is surely not the answer.

Every now and then the administration paraded a group of college students through the prison demonstrating to them what life is like inside a women's prison. It made us feel like animals in a cage. The students walked by, gawking as if looking at zoo attractions. They never made eye contact or stopped to speak to us or ask a question. I don't think they would have been allowed to ask questions if they wanted to. I don't know what the schools thought these students were learning by these rushed walk-throughs. So when a group of Yale law students came I was very excited. Having been a law student, I remembered cherishing the opportunities to talk to people affected by the criminal justice system I was preparing to work in. I rushed to catch up with the students and asked the camp administrator if I, as a former lawyer, could speak with the law students. He told me, "No Goode-James, that's not what they are here for." Still I greeted each student as they walked through the door of our dorm. The students filed past, none of them returning my greeting and most seeming to be even uncomfortable with making eye contact with me. The students walked single file through our tight living quarters. It was strange to have so many new faces in our overcrowded space and none of them acknowledge our presence. Led by the prison administrator the group walked through our living area, including walking unannounced into our bathroom and shower area. We felt angry and resentful. I was shocked that Yale Law School had agreed to this kind of visit.

A more productive visit to the prison may have been for the school to request an opportunity to speak with some of the women in addition to the walk through. They could have had some of the women lead the tour. The prison is not just some building over there. The students' interest in coming to prisons is because of the people that are incarcerated in them. If any of the students had engaged any one of the women they probably would have discovered how very much like them these women were. How they had dreams and goals and also wanted to be happy just like them. If you're ever inclined to visit a prison, which I do hope you do, you're not going to learn much by simply walking through the place. And you make people dislike you. I do not prefer to use the term "assholes", but it's what the women murmured as these folks meandered past us. It's awkward for everyone. How would you feel if someone just stepped unannounced into your bathroom without so much as an introduction? And how do you expect to really learn about the prison experience without speaking to the people involved. Don't you have questions you want to ask?

I spent two consecutive summers and Fourth of July holidays in prison. It was summer time and in the days and evenings leading up to the fourth we could hear the sounds of civilization going on somewhere beyond the prison grounds. We could hear the boats and jet skis on the nearby lake and see people moving about on the mountain range that ran through the area. As it got closer to the fourth the firework displays would start and it was great to see and hear. It would all make me wonder who were these people that lived amongst us, somewhere so close that we could see an occasional rooftop and hear their holiday celebrations, but who never demanded to know who we were or what was going on in this prison.

So this was a really long chapter to say what? The theme of all the encounters I mentioned is the dehumanization and disconnect between people that is acceptable and customary between incarcerated persons and apparently mostly everybody else. I am fascinated with people and their life experiences. What's up with them? Who are they? Everybody has many life stories. How do we expect to find solutions to society's problems without having open dialogue with all parties allowed a seat at the table? People in prison are still the spiritual beings like everyone else, living this lifetime within a human vessel that's allowing us to live out this life's lesson to move us toward our personal and collective greater evolution. They say we all will face a panoramic view of our life when it ends. We will see again each and every experience and encounter we had with another human being. They say that the moon stores our memories. Maybe it can help to remind us before it's too late about our humanity.

BUNKIE

Over-incarceration needs to stop if for no other reason than providing some relief and restoration of human dignity to all the over 40 women in prison and assigned to sleep in upper bunks. At Danbury, if you're 50 or older you get an automatic pass to sleep in the lower bunk and you are known as a lower bunkie. I always wanted to know how did they pick that number. Let me tell you, when it comes to climbing in and out of an upper bunk, there's no difference between forty-five and fifty. But, unless you can get a pass for health reasons, you become an upper bunkie.

I wish I had known that when I came to prison I would be sleeping on a bunk bed, and on the top bunk. I would have interviewed a few four year olds prior to coming here. There's a lot to sleeping in a bunk bed that you don't consider until you're faced with the situation such as negotiating how to get onto the top bunk. Speaking of the ladder, it's a perilous, slippery four rungs of metal. The bottom rung was still too high from the ground for most of us to climb onto so we were provided with metal folding chairs that were just as old and battered as our bunks, to use as stepping stools to the ladders. You have to learn to use your upper body strength to help you ascend and once at the top, learn to throw your leg onto the bunk and hoist your body while holding tight with the foot still on the ladder, while managing to avoid impaling your rib cage. Something that will happen to rookies, but only once.

You learn quickly that it's imperative to create a check list of things you'll need and always refer to before you ascend the ladder because if you forgot something down below it will require another roundtrip on the ladder. Every upper bunkie knows the familiar moan of a fellow upper bunkie who forgot something down below.

Everyone had a bunkie, and yes, we addressed each other as “Bunkie”. Throughout the day as we moved around you gave a special bunkie greeting as you passed each other. As time went by you accumulated former bunkies, but they all still got the bunkie greeting. Unless you hated your bunkie. It happened. Forced to reside in a tiny space the size of the bunk bed you shared, it was a love/hate relationship.

For the most part I liked my bunkies. You learned a lot about a person that you wouldn’t ever get to know about them. I lived with my bunkie, Olympia, the longest. She was one of the most creative and resourceful persons I’ve ever met. She figured out how to make and fix everything with practically nothing. She crotcheted the most beautiful sandals out of shower slippers and we were the only cubicle in C dorm with built in air. She used an old toilet paper box to deflect the air from the fan at the end of the hallway into our cubicle. She was born in a little town in Mexico, eventually came to the U.S., and before going to prison lived in Kentucky with her parents, husband and five children, ages nineteen, eighteen, eight, seven and three. She had been in Danbury for 3.5 years and was serving a 78-month sentence for selling cocaine. She hadn’t seen her children since she’d been there. Her first language was Spanish. She spoke very little English and still each night after working in Unicor she sat on her bunk, her lower bunk, below me, and studied for her G.E.D. for hours.

Some days I wanted to kill her. She constantly fiddled with her locker, laundry bag, and the one thousand plastic and paper bags, scraps of re-used Christmas wrapping paper and just plain old junk she kept rolled up all together. We lived in a space the size of a closet and my bunkie was a hoarder. Every night at around 11:00 and every morning around six, she was up rummaging through her rolls of stuff. Crinkling bags and banging the metal locker doors while illuminating our area with a fluorescent light attached to our bunks that was like the headlights of a car. We lived together in the basement, side by side, with 150 other women. If the roof were removed the scene would resemble a slave ship.

Hanging from the dorm ceilings and from every ceiling in the prison were large, overhead fluorescent lights that remained on until ten at night and were back on every morning at six, except in our cubicle. At the time, I lived in C-2-upper bunk. In our cubicle, lights came on earlier than six a.m. My cubicle was on the side of the dorm that faced the interior of the building. A plastic, frosted window separated my cubicle from the outer hallway above us. Throughout the day and night people walked by banging against the window. Through this window streamed the fluorescent light from the laundry room that started operating at four in the morning. I recently read in an article about how artificial light affects our nervous system. It's all true.

I preferred being an upper bunkie because I felt less closed in within the tight, crowded space we were confined to. I could see things from up there. I kept thinking to my self that once I got home I was going to make a bumper sticker that read, "Upper Bunkies Unite", or "Honk if you were an Upper Bunkie".

Overall I loved all my bunkies. Unfortunately at the time I published this, all except one were still someone's bunkie

THE REAL VOTER FRAUD

One day while sitting up on my bunk looking out over the sea of other upper bunkies, I started thinking it would be great to start organizing the women within the federal prison system into a political action committee to change the harsh sentencing laws that have them serving so much time. Sentencing laws such as disparate crack cocaine mandatory minimums that disproportionately sentence millions of black people to prison for unreasonably long periods of time based on unjustified and unsubstantiated disparities between crack and powder cocaine. I had just read a book by Dr. Rick Hanson titled *Buddha's Brain*. In it he writes, What would it take for everyone to ask what's left out? There's a Zen saying, 'nothing left out.' Nothing left out of your awareness, nothing left out of your practice, nothing left out of your heart. As the circle shrinks, the question naturally arises: what is left out?[xxxvii] This is something that came to mind when I was thinking about getting the women more politically involved. They too are the criminal justice experts who need to be at the policy making table.

Now it's not that I didn't know that all federally incarcerated people and all but two states don't allow incarcerated people to vote while they are physically in a prison, but somehow it didn't register with me that I and the other women in prison were the incarcerated people they were talking about. That happened to me a lot. I was oblivious to how they were categorizing me and unaware that things applied to me. I was aware that when we all returned to our home states we would be subjected to our individual state laws regarding a previously incarcerated person's right to vote but I never really gave any of it much thought.

Voter laws in my state of Massachusetts allow a person to vote once they have been released from a prison, even if on probation or parole. Incarcerated people used to be able to vote in Massachusetts but that changed with a 2009 case called *Simons* v. *Galvin* where prisoners sued the Commonwealth after a referendum stripped incarcerated persons of the right to vote. It all started when a group of incarcerated people decided to create a political action committee to address, as voters, the issue of over-incarceration and the sentencing laws that created it. In response, members of the Massachusetts legislature petitioned for a legislative amendment to the state constitution relative to the right to vote for incarcerated persons. In other words, to strip incarcerated persons of the right to vote so they could not challenge over-incarceration.

On July 29, 1998, the Massachusetts house and the senate met in joint session to vote on the proposal. The Amendment was agreed to with a majority of all members elected having voted in the affirmative.[xxxviii] There were, however, thirty-four state legislators that voted 'Nay' to amending the Constitution to strip incarcerated persons of their right to vote. Senator Diane Wilkerson was one of them. Every black member of the Massachusetts House of Representatives joined her at the time. Senator Wilkerson served sixteen years as the only black female elected to the Massachusetts senate. She happened to be serving a three and a half year federal sentence in Danbury along with me at the time I was writing this so I took advantage of the opportunity to ask her why she voted against this amendment. She told me that she voted against stripping incarcerated persons of the right to vote, "because the Constitution creates inalienable rights for citizens and it should not be used to narrow fundamental rights." In a campaign to raise awareness against the amendment, the Criminal Justice Policy Coalition wrote, "No one has alleged that prisoner voting has harmed our democracy or social fabric…stripping incarcerated felons of their right to vote serves no public safety function…it will not deter crime, repair the harm done by crime, nor help to rehabilitate prisoners."

Anyway, as I mentioned, the proposed amendment was passed by a majority legislative vote. The question then went to the public for vote to make ineligible incarcerated persons to vote in elections for governor, lieutenant governor, secretary of state, state treasurer, state auditor, state attorney general or United States senator or representative in Congress. In other words, if you're locked up, you can't vote. The citizens of Massachusetts passed the referendum 60 to 30 percent, changing the Massachusetts Constitution and stripping convicted incarcerated persons of the right to vote.

The group of prisoner activists pressed on and filed a law suit in federal court claiming the action "violated the Federal Voting Rights Act because it had a disparate impact on the political power of minority voters across Massachusetts, and that it exerted a 'disproportionately adverse effect on the voting rights of African Americans and Hispanic Americans compared to its effect on the voting rights of other citizens because these groups are over-represented in Massachusetts prisons due to considerable racial and ethnic bias, both direct and subtle, in the Massachusetts court system."

The Voting Rights Act of 1965 guaranteed millions of African Americans the right to the electoral franchise. The Act reads, "No voting qualification or prerequisite to voting or standard, practice, or procedure shall be imposed or applied by any State or political subdivision in a manner which results in a denial or abridgement of the right of any citizen of the United States to vote on account of race or color." Since its enactment, the Voting Rights Act was renewed in 1970 for five years, 1975 for seven years, 1982 for 25 years and in 2006 for an additional 25 years. Time is flying by. We had better pay attention.

In defense of the vote to amend the Massachusetts constitution, the Attorney General's office argued that there was no claim that Massachusetts had any history of using laws, rules, practices, tests, or devices to restrict, impede or discourage voting by racial minorities. The first circuit district court upheld the Voting Rights Act claim but it was later denied by the Court of Appeals. Throughout the country different federal circuits were in disagreement about this same issue. Although the 1st, 2nd, and 11th circuits have ruled that the Voting Rights Act does not relate to state laws on incarcerated or ex-incarcerated persons' voter disenfranchisement, in all three of those other circuits, the decisions were not unanimous. One of the then 2nd circuit judges who wrote that the Voting Rights Act does pertain to this issue was now Supreme Court Justice Sonia Sotomayor. In her May 4, 2006 dissenting opinion in *Hayden* v. *Pataki,* which claimed that a New York election law that denied the vote to currently incarcerated people and people on parole, in combination with historic and systematic discrimination in the criminal justice system, violated the Voting Rights Act, 42 U.S.C. Section 1973, Justice Sotomayor wrote, "It is plain to anyone reading the Voting Rights Act that it applies to all voting qualification(s). And it is equally plain that [New York Election Law] section 5-106 [which denies the vote to incarcerated felons and felons on parole] disqualifies a group of people from voting."

Back in Massachusetts, the members of the law suit filed a writ of certiorari urging the United States Supreme Court to clarify which appeals courts had it right. On October 18, 2010, the Supreme Court declined taking up the case. As it stands, incarcerated persons in Massachusetts and most other states are denied the right to vote during their period of incarceration. It doesn't end there.

Nationally, an estimated 5.3 million Americans are denied the right to vote because of laws that prohibit voting by people with felony convictions. That number includes nearly four million who live in thirty-five states that deny people – on probation, parole or those who have completed their sentence – voting rights.[xxxix] In other words, four million, mostly black males, have permanently been stripped of their right to vote. One in every fifty black women in America can no longer vote due to their criminal records.[xl] African American men and women were at least six times more likely than whites to be in prison by the end of 1997.[xli] The potential consequences of these high rates of incarceration for African American men, women, their families and communities are enormous.[xlii] Racial disparities in the criminal justice system result in an estimated thirteen percent of Black men unable to vote.[xliii] Economist Manning Marable referred to the consequence of such widespread disenfranchisement as civil death. He stated that law enforcement and policing policies that target urban communities and residents contribute to this racial disparity that has a direct impact on the process of Black voting.

For any court to uphold the argument put forth by many states that there is no claim that the state has any history of using laws, rules, practices, tests, or devices to restrict, impede, or discourage voting by racial minorities, is to pretend that those states and cities, such as Boston, Massachusetts, has not struggled with a history of race-based practices. Law enforcement policies such as Stop and Frisk and covert restrictive covenants such as the discriminatory housing policies practiced for years by the Boston Housing Authority that denied public housing in certain neighborhoods to Black families. The aggressive saturation of law enforcement targeted at residents of Boston's Black community. Repeated violations of the constitutional protection against unreasonable search and seizure and the countless studies evidencing the harsher treatment and longer sentences given to Black defendants in the Commonwealth's courts. The stripping of voting rights is seriously impacting the very urban areas where a healthy electorate is most needed in order to effect change quickly, and the number of low-income minority citizens losing their right to self-determination is continuing to grow like the number of hamburgers sold at McDonalds. If this trend continues at the current rate, it is estimated that forty percent of the next generation of black men will not have the right to vote.[xliv]

Voter disenfranchisement laws expand upon the narrow view that has proven to be an ineffective model of addressing breaches of the law. It's more of taking a broad brush in defining a person solely by their offense. Even during a period of incarceration a person has other aspects of their life, such as parenthood, that vests in them a political interest. There are numerous ballot issues that impact the lives of families of the incarcerated and this most definitely refers to the actual laws that place people in prisons who would be better off receiving drug rehabilitation and other forms of alternatives to incarceration within the communities they live. While in Danbury Prison I knew women who served long sentences for drugs who, within a few months of being released, returned to prison on probation violations due to drug use. Who better than drug addicts to help carve out and enact legislation that would be effective in stopping the revolving door of recidivism due to drug addiction? Voter disenfranchisement keeps in place a failed forty year war on drugs and further erodes the electorate in the communities where voting is most needed and increases the power in the hands of the few.

And now the evil empire has moved beyond targeting people within the criminal justice system and has pounced upon the remaining poor people. Everyday we hear about more states enacting voter identity laws that are professed to have been created to stop voter fraud. According to the Brennan Center for Justice, allegations of widespread fraud by malevolent voters are easy to make, but often prove to be inflated or inaccurate…These claims are frequently used to justify policies – including restrictive photo identification rules – that could not solve the alleged wrongs, but that could well disenfranchise legitimate voters.[xlv] At this rate it wouldn't take much when the time comes around again to renew the Voting Rights Act that there may not be enough votes to make it happen.

Monique Williams, Rhonda Turpin, Tia Bills, Arlinda 'Trey' Johns, and I did start an organization while at Danbury and it still exists today. Families for Justice as Healing. www.justiceashealing.org. We are a legislative advocacy group and we advocate for harm reduction, community-based wellness initiatives to replace incarceration. We speak from the perspective of incarcerated women and our children. We ask for justice as healing and, yes, we sell dishcloths to fund our organization and contribute to a bridge employment fund for mothers coming home from prison. Please visit our website often and buy some.

CAN'T VOTE YET STILL COUNTED

The United States Census Bureau is an agency of the Commerce Department and is responsible for the Census that is the official count of people made for the purpose of compiling social and economic data for the political subdivisions to which people belong. The census count generates population figures that are used to apportion seats in the U.S. House of Representatives and to distribute currently more than four hundred billion in federal aid. The census is taken every ten years and is conducted by a head count via mail and door-to-door canvassing.

For purposes of the U.S. Census, because incarcerated people are counted as residents of the prison towns, many sparsely populated areas become additional political districts due to the prison population. I was incarcerated in the federal prison camp for women in Danbury, Connecticut during the 2010 high stakes census. Danbury has been ranked Safest City in Connecticut. In 2010, the median income for a family was $61, 899 as opposed to the $28,574 median income for my hometown of Roxbury.

I lived in my beloved community of Roxbury, Massachusetts all of my life. Roxbury is a black community rich with a history of socially conscious activism and generations of families that have remained committed to the neighborhood and to our youth and their education. A profoundly disappointing moment for me during my incarceration was the day we were all put in lock-down while the officers passed out to us 2010 census forms. We were instructed to fill in our names only. We were told that the rest would be filled out for us. Part of that meant that the officers would fill out the address section on the census forms to reflect our residence as the prison location, instead of for instance, Roxbury where I had lived all of my life and where my husband, children, parents and home were. I felt sick to know that I would be counted as a resident of Danbury,

Connecticut. I pictured all the faces of black children sitting in schools in my district desperate for money and resources. This was a painful realization for me. I asked if I could opt out of filling out my census form. I was told that not filing a census form is a federal offense. I wondered if it were a federal offense for corrections officers to tamper with a census form belonging to another person.

Around the same time that we were locked up trying to defend what we believed should be our right to be counted as residents of our home communities, on April 12, 2010, the state of Maryland became the first state in the country to count incarcerated people as residents of their hometowns, rather than as residents of the place where they were imprisoned. In Maryland, for purposes of legislative redistricting, the passage of No representation Without Population Act ended prison-based gerrymandering, which falsely inflated the political power of districts with prisons, due to the U.S. Census Bureau's practice of counting incarcerated populations as residents of the prison.[xlvi]

At the same time Black groups urged government to improve the count of African-Americans in the 2010 census, saying that they won't be satisfied with a tally that has historically overlooked millions in their community. According to the Associated Press, the National Urban League, the NAACP, Rev. Al Sharpton and Rev. Jesse Jackson met with Commerce Secretary Gary Locke to voice their concerns that the Census Bureau might not be doing enough to ensure an accurate tally. About three million blacks were missed in 2000, while many whites were over-counted. The leaders went on to say they wanted to see a change in how the government tallies prisoners, so they are counted as residents of the cities in which they previously lived, not where a prison is located. There are practical political consequences of the mass incarceration of black Americans. In New York State, for example, the prison populations play a significant role in how some state legislative districts are drawn up. In New York's 45th senatorial district, located in the extreme northern corner of upstate New York, there are thirteen state prisons, with fourteen thousand prisoners, all of whom are counted as residents of that district. Prisoners in New York are disenfranchised – they cannot vote- yet their numbers help to create a Republican state senatorial district. These "prison districts" now exist all over the United States.[xlvii]

Too often the issue of correcting political gerrymandering has been mischaracterized as an urban-versus-rural issue. It is not. It needs to be corrected for electoral equality and fair representation. Back in my hometown few people paid attention to an October 2011 article in our local paper, The Bay State Banner, which reported that members of a coalition of Massachusetts organizations are calling on the Massachusetts Redistricting Committee to refrain from counting prison populations in the drawing of districts. Currently, the Massachusetts Constitution prevents the Committee from changing the way incarcerated people are counted. Clearly this is an issue where some members of the Massachusetts legislature need to petition for another legislative amendment to the state's constitution.

THE MISSING SEAT AT THE TABLE

The problem in this country with its history of criminal justice policy making is what Harvard Law School Professor Lonnie Guiner refers to as the missing seats at the table. Those people who have the actual life experience of those being judged. You cannot serve in public office if you have been convicted of a felony. We have a United States Sentencing Commission that does not have any members that have experienced incarceration. The stories I would hear from women I was in prison with reminded me of the importance of inclusion in decision-making and to always keep the human factor as part of the equation.

I already mentioned in a previous chapter that I lived in C dorm. A typical night in C dorm would consist of young women piled up in the cubicle two doors down from me talking about their latest episodes, all beginning and ending with “motherfucking bitches”. My bunkie, Olympia, often would be belting out Mexican love ballads and the late night crew, the group that started hanging out by the microwave area every night after 10:00 pm count, even though they took the microwaves from us weeks ago, began telling their stories. Ms. Annie was 70 years old and the noise often got her confused and disorientated. When things really kicked in she would walk around clutching her bible and stand in the doorway trying to decide where to go to get away from the noise. And that’s what it would sound like on the surface. Just noise. But listen closely and you would hear the life stories of women who were not just crude and offensive. You would hear the personal stories of survivors and clever, loving, creative women who had survived amidst unbelievable odds that they were up against all the time.

As I lay on my bunk listening to the conversations going on around me the one recurring thought I had was who created this phenomenon and how did they come up with this as a way to punish people. Throw too many people in a too small space and make them all live together. How did they determine how long a person should stay in prison? What formula did they use? The decision makers obviously did not include anyone who had the experience of existing in a prison. It reminded me of the anger I felt while sitting in my first year law school constitutional law class when we read the Supreme Court cases upholding slavery and the property rights of slaveholders. I raised my hand often and tried to interject something into the conversation that acknowledged that we were lauding the decision making process of people who donned robes and performed as judges while never addressing the human factor. Except for my contracts law professor, David Hall, who happened to also be the dean of the law school and a black man, who on the first day of contracts when introducing us to the early cases made it clear to us that unlike as described in the case law, we were reading about people, not property. Black people held in bondage and treated like cattle. It seemed a lot like our treatment as incarcerated people as provided for by the 13th Amendment of the United States Constitution.

The exclusion of the human factor and the missing chair at the policy making table continues today resulting in cases like *Harmelin v. Michigan*. Ronald Harmelin was convicted under Michigan law of possessing more than 650 grams of cocaine and sentenced to a mandatory term of life in prison without possibility of parole. He appealed his sentence to the Supreme Court claiming that the sentence was cruel and unusual because it was "significantly disproportionate" to the crime he committed, and because the sentencing judge was statutorily required to impose it, without taking into account the particularized circumstances of the crime and of the criminal. The Eighth Amendment states, excessive bail shall not be required, nor excessive fines imposed, nor cruel and unusual punishments inflicted. On June 27, 1991, Supreme Court Justice Scalia stated that "Severe, mandatory penalties may be cruel, but they are not unusual in the constitutional sense, having been employed in various forms throughout the Nation's history. Mr. Harmelin was to remain in prison for the rest of his life for being in possession of 650 grams of cocaine.

In his dissenting opinion, Justice Byron R. White said that while drugs were a serious societal problem, such a "harsh mandatory penalty should be applied only to crimes that always warrant that punishment. He said, "To be constitutionally proportionate, punishment must be tailored to a defendant's personal responsibility and moral guilt." Justices Harry A. Blackmun and John Paul Stevens joined Justice White's dissent. Justice Stevens also filed a separate dissenting opinion, as did Justice Thurgood Marshall.[xlviii] (New York Times*)*. Justice Scalia's opinion was a purely interpretist constitutional analysis that excluded all relative human factors and upheld a sentence of life in prison for a first-time offender convicted for possessing drugs.

On October 6, 2010, almost twenty years after the Supreme Court's decision in *Harmelin*, Retired Supreme Court Justice John Paul Stephens gave a speech at the National Legal Aid & Defender Association Exemplar Award Dinner. He used the entire time of his speech to talk about the *Harmelin* decision. Here is an excerpt from Justice Stephen's speech that night:

The case that I plan to discuss tonight may not be as interesting as a Shakespeare play, but it does shed some light on the role of history in the judicial process. It was argued in November of 1990 and decided on June 27, 1991, the last day of the Term. It was a five-to-four decision; two opinions supporting the judgment and the three dissenting opinions. The name of the case is Harmelin v. Michigan, 501 U.S. 957

(1991). Harmelin, a first-time offender, was convicted of possession of over 650 grams of a mixture containing cocaine. As a cloistered appellate judge, I have never seen cocaine myself, but I understand that the quantity actually possessed by Harmelin – 672 grams, or a little less than a pound and a half – could have been carried around in a brown paper bag or concealed in a glove compartment. Pursuant to Michigan law, he received a mandatory sentence of life imprisonment without the possibility of parole. Under the statute the same sentence would have been imposed regardless of whether he was a kingpin in a major drug cartel or merely a part-time messenger hired to make one delivery. The question presented to the Court was whether that sentence constituted cruel and unusual punishment within the meaning of the federal constitution. The Court held that it did not.

Justice Stephens could have talked about any number of cases or issues he presided over while a judge in the highest court in the land. He chose to speak about a case where a man, never even arrested before, was sentenced to live the rest of his life in prison without the possibility of parole for possessing some cocaine. The Michigan law was part of the harsh drug sentencing legislation crafted by the American Legislative Exchange Council, a conservative right wing membership that introduces legislation to the states through republican legislators.

In February 2012, I spoke with Attorney Carla Johnson who was the attorney for Mr. Harmelin at the Supreme Court level. She had known Mr. Harmelin in Detroit for years prior to his arrest and subsequent life sentence with no parole for possession of cocaine. He was the deskman at a pool hall and she described him as a "great guy…the nicest guy you know." Johnson said she thinks about Mr. Harmelin all the time. Johnson said that during oral arguments, Justice Scalia commented that Michigan's law may be cruel, but it was not unusual. Unlike the United States Constitution that read cruel *and* unusual punishment, the Michigan constitution did not allow for cruel *or* unusual punishment, allowing for an inroad back to state court where it was argued that because Justice Scalia said that the law was cruel, it violated the Michigan state constitution. Eventually the law was repealed and after serving 13 years in a Michigan prison Ronald Harmelin was released along with other people in that state who were serving the "650-lifer law", punishment for possessing more than 650 grams of cocaine or heroin. After being released from prison Harmelin landed a construction job but died of a heart attack 6 months after his release. This was the type of case exemplifying women all around me. Good decent women who didn't need to spend another minute in prison, were in for many years. Mostly survival offenders. Casualties of the drug war and a contrived plan of social control that from my vantage point from atop my prison bunk was hugely successful. It absolutely was cruel, but as Justice Scalia stated, not unusual.

For months after my release from prison I was on home-confinement and had to check in to the halfway house every Thursday. Checking in meant meeting with my case manager, who was younger than my oldest daughter, and recounting to her all the jobs I applied for that week but didn't get, then finishing up by being watched as I peed in a cup to provide my weekly urine sample, even though my case had nothing to do with drug use. If all of that didn't fill up the hour check-in time I had to sit in the common area of the halfway house for the remainder of the time until I was given permission to leave. At times waiting around was like a family reunion because I would run into women I knew from the prison who had just been released to the halfway house. In addition to federal women, the halfway house also housed women from the county jail who had violated their probation for one reason or another, mostly for relapsing into drug use, and were sent back to the halfway house for a period of time. Most of those women had been through the place like a revolving door.

One of the women I really enjoyed seeing at the halfway house was Curley. Curley was a white woman from South Boston who had been battling a heroin addiction for more than 20 years. She was also one of the funniest people I've ever met. Nothing could keep her true spirit from exploding onto the scene whenever she told her stories. She told me about the ins and outs of addiction and what works and what doesn't. One day she told me, "I'm tired. I'm 46 years old. I've been a drug addict for more than 20 years. Do you know what it's like to stand in front of a judge at my age with a sex-for-a-fee charge? It's embarrassing. I'm tired". Curley personified for me what shamans and spiritual healers teach us about drug addiction. Although addicts get stuck in addiction, they are seekers of their true spirit trying to alter their present state of mind to enter that true state of consciousness. Curley could tell you about everything that worked and didn't work that has being offered for drug treatment. Later, as I became more involved with my organization, Families for Justice as Healing, and advocated for harm reduction alternatives to the war on drugs and drug prohibition, I would be at many planning tables where people with Curley's expertise weren't included. It's the Curleys who need to be a part of the conversation and planning for criminal justice policies and effective drug treatment.

We are inundated with pharmaceutical industry commercials for the latest cures produced by the Nation's leading drug companies. Today there's a pill for everything. Legal drugs. Illegal drugs. Legal painkillers that simulate an illegal drug high. It's enough to make you crazy. And then they'll put you on some drug for that. The takeaway is that they are all drugs that people use to alleviate pain somehow, someway. Physical pain; emotional pain; pain we don't know was pain. It goes on and on.

The majority of the people consuming illegal and legal drugs in this country do so in a controlled manner without falling off that cliff into addiction. People have been using mind-altering substances since the beginning of time. Our college campuses, professional work places, Wall Street and the military are full of social drug users and social users are the majority of drug consumers, the ones that dramatically increase the never-ending demand for the supply. In June 2011 the Substance Abuse and Mental Health Services Administration released its annual report that detailed its findings of a survey of illegal drug use in the United States. Based on 67,500 people, surveyed since 2002, it is considered the most comprehensive annual snapshot of drug use in the U.S. While cocaine abuse continues to decline, with use of the drug down thirty two percent from its peak in 2006, about 21.8 million Americans, or 8.7 percent of the population age 12 and older, reported using illegal drugs in 2009. The previous high was just over twenty million users in 2006. Because they are legal, this study did not include the dangerous drugs of alcohol and cigarettes that cause more deaths per year than any illegal drugs. Tobacco kills a total of 5.7 million people worldwide each year and second-hand smoke kills more than 600,000 people each year.[xlix]

There is no end to the ways chemicals are manipulated to create various forms of substances. More and more, unlike drugs such as cocaine and heroin that are grown in far off places drugs, like crystal meth, can be made from household products. The only essential ingredient in meth is ephedrine or pseudoephedrine, a widely used over-the-counter decongestant used to relieve nasal congestion caused by colds, allergies, and hay fever. More and more drugs are being made from household products. There is even a federal agency now assigned to maintaining a lab to try and reverse engineer drugs as they are discovered so that that can be identified and made illegal. Legislation is now pending to take steps to curb illegal methamphetamine production. The Combat Methamphetamine Enhancement Act would require retailers of pseudoephedrine and ephedrine products to verify that they have met the requirements of the Combat Methamphetamine Epidemic Act. Of course, the powerful pharmaceutical industry has mounted a strong lobby against the proposed regulatory legislation. Law enforcement chasing drugs and the current method of incarceration as the way to address the use and sale of drugs will never be effective.

The war on drugs hasn't worked for stopping the creation, sale or use of illegal drugs for forty years and it's not just going to suddenly kick in and be effective in stopping drug abuse. The war on drugs is not about that. If it were we would be asking people why they get high and what they need to live quality lives. What we need is effective treatment for those who are suffering from addiction illnesses because the drugs are never going to go away. As Clifford Thornton, the founder of Efficacy and an international expert and long time crusader of drug policy reform states, "what we need is to bring illegal drugs inside the law and begin the real work of shifting the distribution of wealth to address and support the basic human needs of quality health care, housing and education for all people…We must start looking at the city police budgets across the country and at the prison budgets and taking a serious look at the economics of this". We should look at new legal frameworks such as legalization as advocated by Law Enforcement Against Prohibition (LEAP), an organization with a membership of law enforcement, prosecutors and judges who demand an immediate end to the drug war and to legalize all drugs. Or there's the option of decriminalization as enacted by

Portugal. As reported by Glenn Greenwald in a report by the CATO Institute, *Drug Decriminalization In Portugal: Lessons For Creating Fair And Successful Drug Policies,* in July of 2001 Portugal decriminalized, not legalized, all drugs and drug possession for personal use and drug usage itself are still legally prohibited, but violations of those prohibitions are deemed to be exclusively administrative violations and are removed from the criminal realm. Drug trafficking continues to be prosecuted as a criminal offense.

Most important, when we examine how to create these more successful policies, the experts that should be at the table are those who know first hand what works and how best to find solutions that don't exact punishment spanning life times and further devastate families and communities.

MEDIA INFLUENCE

Sometimes when I was in prison I would watch the news and get totally swept up into a symphony of ooohs and aaahs at the news on the television. On this particular morning, for instance, the story that got us all going was about a little boy who brought to his elementary school 18 packets of heroin. His father accidentally left it within his reach.

The hysteria stirred up by the flash news story broadcasted over a tri-state area, was an example of the media's contribution to sustaining the unreasonable criminal justice drug sentencing policies. The difference here was that many of the women watching that news story had been sitting in this prison for similar drug-related offenses, as first time, non-violent offenders, who had been separated from their children for years. Here were actual examples of what were probable outcomes for that child's parent winding up in court somewhere, formally charged with as many violations of state law that could be made to fit. Subsequently, they would ultimately wind up yet another person sitting in a prison. Taxpayers will put out on average, $45.00 per day for that father to sit in a cell. His son will be sent back to the school where, in kindergarten, he will sit in a classroom with about twenty other children. A disproportionate percentage of them will contribute to the 2.5 million children in the United States, with one or both parents incarcerated. Yet another missed opportunity for the use of evidence based, harm-reduction, community wellness initiatives, while helping a family to heal. A news story flashed over a tri-state area, stirring up feelings of judgment, blame, disgust, anger, hatred, in those who sit in their homes creating their reality for that day through the experience of television. Television culminates and reinforces the canopy of collective thought when it tells its stories, and we see them happening before our eyes. In this sense, the television has literally become our window on the world. What we observe on the screen becomes a sort of first-hand experience.[l]

We begin to associate those feelings of judgment, blame, disgust, anger, and hatred, with our collective wellbeing. We are all connected by our energy and particularly the energy of anger. Blame and fear allow us to dismiss those of us who fit the description of the parent we imagined as that story was being broadcast. An elementary school student brought 18 packets of heroin to school. This bit of information causes us to compartmentalize people in categories of worthiness and unworthiness. This is the energy that is massed produced among us. This is the energy that is gelling within our communities and its impact is causing our society to suffer. Every time we submit to this desire for vengeance, every time we dehumanize people, we lose something of our own spirit and dignity.[li]

It is that feeling of contentment and happiness that watching the news helps us to accomplish just enough on our own surface to keep us content with our lives and life styles. The problem exists when that sense of contentment is motivated by the feeling of “I’m o.k. but you are not.” We hate drug addicts. We despise the parent that had a household where a young child could get hold to bags of heroin. Yet I sat next to women who had experiences with drugs while parenting and they in no way fit the mental media image of that “terrible parent” created by a flash news story. The constant barrage of judgment, fear-based sensationalized news stories keeps our minds cluttered and disturbed with the noise of judgment and punishment instead of opportunity for effective solution. These quick infusions of hate – judgment energy are how we begin to respond to encounters in general. Our conversations become mostly focused around bad situations and complaining. This type of energy increases its frequency within and around us, clouding our minds and our senses. A media barrage of this information disturbs our mind and if your mind is not calm, never steady, on a minute-by-minute basis, you cannot see the situation for what it is. Instead, you see what your hatred-judgment energy projects into it. Research tells us that the vast majority of us – ninety-five percent - shape our impression of crime and criminal justice primarily from the mass media, of which television is easily the most influential.[lii] In other words, whatever it is that we believe about crime, right or wrong, we likely have the owners of media to thank.[liii] You, as well as others, will see the big picture, but few will care about the politics of crime and its role in our growing prison population. You will know that most prisoners are guilty of breaking the law. You will not know that only a few need to be separated from society. You will know that it is the reporting and sensationalism of crime that has skyrocketed. You will be unaware that crime itself has not.[liv]

A total revolution in physics has occurred since 1900 that is reflected by what's in our minds and what's going on in the world. Yet most people do not understand this breakthrough.[lv] Our third dimensional world is adrift in all the things the new physics has invented – television, computers, microwave ovens and cell phones – yet people don't know how these things work.[lvi] This is interesting stuff. Clever media manipulate the collective mind to make money and control our ability for critical thinking.

There are studies that demonstrate that there are things called mirror neurons. They are mechanisms in our brain that come to attention when we observe someone doing something or expressing an emotion. According to Stephen Kiesling in his article, *Do False TV Memories Make Our World Extra Frightening,* false memories can be created by watching TV. The article discusses whether false television memories increase people's anxiety about the world. Research conducted at Jacobs University in Bremen,

Germany indicates that the mechanism for false memories could be triggered by mirror neurons. Mirror neurons simulate actions or emotions that humans observe in others and are thought to be the basis of empathy, which allows humans to feel another's joy and pain.[lvii] Keisling explains to us that, speculating further, the more emotionally charged scenes on TV – the crime and brutal violence, for example – are likely the ones that most powerfully trigger our mirror neurons, and are perhaps most likely to become embedded in our memories. This could help account for studies showing that people who watch more television are significantly more fearful about the outside world than those who watch less. It may also explain why fear of crime has risen even as crime rates fall.[lviii]

The hunt for the story is intense. Today, just a few of the wealthiest media corporations control every form of communication known to mankind. Heavily invested in ownership of the ever-changing technologies that bring us the news, these communication tools, while inundating us with messages of fear, hate and buy, buy, buy, are also being used to gather information about us. According to Free Press, a national, nonpartisan, nonprofit organization working to reform the media, the U.S. media landscape is dominated by massive corporations that, through a history of mergers and acquisitions, have concentrated their control over what we see, hear and read. As Free Press explains to us, in many cases, these giant companies are vertically integrated, controlling everything from initial production to final distribution. On the Free Press website they provide us with a chart of the Big Six, Cable, TV, Print, Telecom and Radio. The big six are General Electric, Walt Disney, Rupert Murdoch's News Corp, Time Warner, Viacom and CBS. Today, even as the largest media mogul, Rupert Murdoch, was on the brink of purchasing one of the largest broadcast companies, his print media empire is under investigation after being exposed for using criminal wire tapping tactics to create news stories. The big six deliver to us everything we receive regarding news, entertainment, and what we need to buy. They create everyday experiences that our mirror neurons make us believe are our own and shape what we think and feel.

A healthy media story could have been told by holding off on the story of the young boy with the packets of heroin until there was some productive resolution to the matter. How different would viewers' responses be if, for example, stories involving at-risk children and families started with reporting on the work of places like the Youth Advocacy Division.

I worked at the Youth Advocacy Division (YAD), part of the public defender agency in Massachusetts. YAD, formerly referred to as the Youth Advocacy Project, began in 1992 with a goal of protecting and advancing the legal and human rights of children and promoting their healthy development. The mission of the YAD is to ensure that every child in Massachusetts has access to zealous legal representation. YAD provides not just legal advocacy to court involved children but also provides comprehensive representation and resources to prevent further court involvement. They ask the human questions. Who is this little boy walking around with packets of heroin in his pocket? Where does he go to school and how is he doing in school? What is his school attendance like and how is he performing academically? Does he have siblings? Is he well nourished? What is his relationship with his parents? Are they court-involved? Are they struggling or in crisis in their own lives? At YAD they get an accurate portrait of who the child and family are. YAD is not simply a flash of human dysfunction and frailty sensationalized under the media-scope intended to get our heads shaking at the television. YAD is not designed to feed our imaginations and conjure up more images that produce fear and judgment. It is not meant to support the hard line punishment and unproductive responses that do prevail in the media. The Youth Advocacy Division is an example of an evidence-based, community project that addresses justice for children and families from a place of healing. The Youth Advocacy Division is an example of the kind of community wellness resource available if we committed to a shift in paying out billions of dollars for law enforcement and mass incarceration in furtherance of failed drug policies.

I did see a healthy media story on PBS. It showed a successful approach to the addiction illness of alcohol. It was about a wet house in Seattle, Washington, paid for by tax dollars. A wet house is a residential facility where chronic homeless alcoholics live for free, drink freely, and have access to a complete array of health and alcohol treatment programs. It is a community for the chronic alcoholic who would otherwise be struggling everyday to live on the streets. In a wet house the resident is allowed to drink freely while being provided a clean, safe place to live. Most of the men living in the wet house at the time of the news story were actively engaged in programs to help them with their addiction to alcohol. In most cases the programs were working. It wasn't working for everyone at the same time. One resident even died during the filming of the story from alcohol related illness. But being in that community, with daily living needs being met, the men were freed from the disorienting pressures of trying to find food and shelter while being chronic alcoholics. Health care, employment, civic responsibilities, parental responsibilities were issues that there was no room for when living on the streets. Having a safe, clean place to live started most of them on the road to recovery.

The concept of the wet house as a solution started at the root cause of the problem of alcoholism. It began unpacking the layers of trauma from the root of the sickness. It did so by allowing the person to drink. One of the residents described living in the wet house as an experience that provided him with an environment that for the first time in years allowed him to see the impact that drinking had on his life. Not just see it, but also feel it. For the first time he was able to sit back and look at his situation without having to jump into the bottle to escape the most immediate pain confronting him at the moment.

When people are barely surviving there is little room for clear, thinking. Barely surviving breeds fear and a poverty mentality. Poverty mentality cuts off the energy and life force within a person creating walls stronger than any physical barriers man could perceive. Add a chemical dependency to that and daily living issues become so immediate it doesn't allow the person to explore the reasons for their pain and self-medication. As in the wet house, once the living standards were brought up to quality level coupled with excellent programming, it provided the men the space and tools to begin to unravel the true depth of their relationship with alcohol and they began to heal.

Media induced fear has caused our reasoning minds to fail when it comes to criminal justice. More than half of the prison population is non-violent offenders. Most are under-educated and unskilled for today's employment opportunities. Many are themselves victims of physical and emotional abuse. The response to this is to warehouse them in prisons for years. They are offered little to no substance abuse or mental health treatment. Substantive educational programs are non-existent. We must come out of the false T.V. memories that shape our current experiences and begin to engage in the truths about the lives of real people.

THE MONEY PIT

In addition to overly punitive and disparate sentencing policies, voter disenfranchisement, bogus voting districts and the barrage of fear based media, special interest group money contributes significantly to a business boom based on mass incarceration. The definition of lobby is (1) to talk with or curry favor with a legislator, usu. repeatedly or frequently, in an attempt to influence the legislator's vote. (2) To support or oppose (a measure) by working to influence a legislator's vote, i.e., the organization lobbied the bill through the senate. (3) To try to influence (a decision-maker), i.e., the lawyer lobbied the judge for a favorable ruling.[lix] – *Black's Law Dictionary, ninth edition.* There are state and federal laws such as the federal regulation of Lobbying Act, 12 USCA section 261, that govern the conduct of lobbyists by requiring them to register and file activity reports, as well as regulates how campaigns are financed. These laws still have very little overall impact on how money affects politics.

Political action committees (PACs) are organizations formed by special-interest groups to raise and contribute money to the campaigns of political candidates who the group believes will promote its interests. PACs distribute contributions on behalf of companies, labor unions and others with common economic interests.

The modern way campaigns are now financed in American politics creates long and winding money trails often shuffled around like a shell game involving lawmakers turned lobbyists and then back again to lawmakers, and the rules vary from state to state. Alabama for example has the most permissive campaign finance rules in the country allowing contributions of unlimited size from individuals and corporations. Getting around campaign finance laws are up to the creativity of those collecting the funds.

Special interest group money does far more than put candidates in office. At times it has even gravely impacted the principle of judicial independence. Large sums of money are raised by local and national interest groups to support or oppose issues that are important to those groups. Judges who make rulings consistent with the constitutions, adhering to the principle of judicial independence, could easily find themselves unseated from the bench if certain decisions are not in-line with the ideologies of the powerful special interest groups. Millions of Dollars are spent on television and radio advertising for both political candidates and issues to convince voters of what they should support. And Americans most often follow the constant message as opposed to doing their own homework.

So too does special interest spending boost lobbying efforts in attempts to counter pending government regulations on corporations. As new safety and protective regulations are proposed that affect industries from textiles to finance, those industries increase their lobbying efforts to influence Washington policy. Two thousand lobbyists registered this year to lobby for the financial industry (that's almost four lobbyists for every member of the House and Senate). The imbalance can be measured not just in bodies but also in the unending flow of alternative-language proposals and extravagant white papers that the heavy hitters churned out.[lx] With the pouring in of PAC money into campaign contributions, hiring of lobbyists, and the funding of the churning out of white paper, the written findings that bolster lobbyists' positions and are distributed to lawmakers, you begin to see how special interest money affects the laws that govern this country and its citizens. The interests of groups that are not supported by powerful PACs with big money are increasingly being silenced along with the legislation that is meaningful to their survival.

In the United States Supreme Court's recent decision in

Citizens United v. *Federal Election Commission*, the Court held that the government cannot limit corporate political spending in elections because such a limit would restrict political speech. So now, corporations are able to spend their profits on TV ads urging voters to vote for or against a candidate or an issue. As a result of the Supreme's Court's decision in *Citizens*, corporations have the power to pour money into elections and provide millions of dollars to pay for political activity. Millions of dollars for political media blitzes touting the interests of wealthy individuals and their special interest groups and ultimately bankrolling the work of Congress. Business interests have found a receptive audience under Chief Justice John G. Roberts, Jr. and the current Supreme Court has consistently upheld the rights and power of corporations while eroding the individual rights of defendants.

Before *Citizens,* twenty-four states restricted corporate spending on elections. After *Citizens*, twenty-three of them stopped enforcing their corporate finance laws. This is significant in regards to the influence of how we are governed considering that the vast majority of elections are on the state and local level. This onslaught of special-interest money puts republicans in office with the republican agenda of making a relentless attack on civil rights advancements and initiatives to turn the clock back on progress in the area of civic engagement among people of color in this country. Much of the money has gone toward the on-going political realignment that has been taking place for decades, since the 1960's civil rights legislation when southern whites fled the Democratic Party, aimed at shifting white southern democrats to the Republican Party. Millions of special interest dollars have gone to "leaving republicans at a stronger position in the south than at any time since reconstruction.[lxi]

The spending of millions of dollars, to help conservative,

republican candidates and further the interests of some three million businesses is rivaled only by support for a burgeoning prison industry. When it comes to incarcerating people and the creation of the laws that define crime and determine sentencing, it may be legal for prison industry PACS and lobbyists to line the pockets of law makers, but it is wrong to create a prison system that generates billions of private sector dollars from the creation of laws that incarcerate people for unreasonably long periods of time. Mostly poor people of color who are marginalized and herded like cattle into and through the maze of the criminal justice behemoth consisting of police, prosecutors and crime created out of issues related to economic inequality and poverty.

Special interest money has sponsored the conservative political agenda that performs as a social justice devouring machine. There are many examples of such legislation. Republican governors have stripped education budgets of millions of dollars while increasing budgets for prisons. Emergency Manager Laws have been used in financially troubled communities to get around local elections in the guise of fixing the debt. Voter I.D. and voter disenfranchisement laws; laws enacted to eliminate collective bargaining; Stand Your Ground Laws; and of course, mandatory minimum sentencing laws.

Our current state of affairs requires that we save ourselves from the aggressive multinational corporate takeover of our politics, technology and natural resources. Consumption is occurring at a dizzying pace and so too is our environment showing the signs of this. We need an army of young, bright minds ready with solutions on how to resuscitate ourselves and our planet from the onslaught of environmental, health and financial problems caused by the elite power controlling groups. Such young minds could help us shift from the greed and wasteful consumption of the current banking and commodities industries that have left the masses bewildered and bankrupt. We have no idea which one of our children will become doctor, scientist or economist, the savior at the right time. Whether it be a child educated in Harlem School District 122 or one of the students sitting in a classroom in the bankrupt Chester Upland District in Pennsylvania who only continues to receive an education because the teachers continue to show up and teach with no pay.

As far back as the late 1800s, upon leaving the U.S. Presidency, Rutherford B. Hayes wrote in his diary: "The real difficulty is with the vast wealth and power in the hands of the few…It is government of the people, by the people, and for the people no longer. It is government of corporations, by corporations and for corporations." Apparently these increasingly common state-by-state enactments of legislation are far more sinister and intentional than realized. A nefarious and quietly constructed master plan is in the hands of organizations such as the National Rifle Association and the far too long inconspicuous group known as the American Legislative Exchange Council (ALEC).

I was running on the track one day, an activity I did as much as I could while incarcerated. Eventually it turned into a 5-mile-a-day jog. Anything to keep me outside in the fresh air and alleviate the angst of the everyday monotony of prison was life sustaining for me. Anyway, I often listened to National Public Radio while running and on this day NPR had a story about ALEC. It had been exposed through a leak of pages and pages of documents that turned out to be model legislation. I had already been following ALEC closely by having family and friends search for articles about it after I stumbled over a newspaper article that mentioned ALEC's position on private prisons. I had learned that its public safety task force had drafted legislation to be used by its membership of republican state legislators to increase private prisons.

I was stunned to learn that for years ALEC has been behind some of the most damaging criminal justice legislation passed. For example, years ago, ALEC members, including the National Rifle Association, modeled legislation and launched media campaigns funded by the NRA, that ultimately led to states adopting mandatory minimum sentencing and, more recently, laws that have shut down any meaningful civil litigation against the gun industry. Laws such as the Protection of Lawful Commerce in Arms Act of 2005 and the Tiahrt Amendment. The NRA reflects a certain part of American Culture… It's conservative and they're frightened by all the demographic changes of the past half-century… They see guns as a way to fight back against people who are different. [lxii] I was intrigued to find that such an organization had positioned itself to have the depth of influence on state level sentencing legislation throughout the country as well. Conservative, republican, copycat legislation that popped up in state after state. Prior to hearing NPR's story, I had been reading everything I could about ALEC because I was trying to figure out how I could grow my organization, Families for Justice as Healing, working with socially conscious legislators and corporations. I couldn't think of an existing organization like this that mass-produced legislation working on the side of the people.

NPR's story on the American Legislative Exchange Council was based on the Center for Media and Democracy and its procurement of eight hundred ALEC model bills. They referred to this coup as "ALEC Exposed". According to NPR, the American Legislative Exchange Council brings together state legislators with corporations to draft model legislation. There are over 2,000 legislative members. The main goal is to draft model legislation and resolutions. These are based on an ideology that focuses on advancement via an agenda of multinational corporations to clear the way for ultra conservative action. ALEC wants protections against lawsuits, such as tort law reform. ALEC champions privatization, including public education in the form of voucher programs. ALEC privatizes prisons using business models such as Corrections Corporation of America (CCA). This is the largest provider of private prisons and a very active member of ALEC.

ALEC focused on the state level, as that's where there is contact with government on a regular basis. For example, state and local government have the biggest hand in public education. ALEC describes itself as a non-profit membership group, not a lobbyist group. Individual legislators become members at a cost of $50.00 and corporations pay $7,000 - $25,000 to join. Corporations also pay additional fees to be on task forces with legislators. Corporations have veto power. Once the model legislation is drafted legislators carry it back to their states. This creates uniformity in legislation within the states. The documents obtained by the Center for Media and Democracy gave examples of model legislation from ALEC that covered limiting taxing ability of states on corporations; tort reform; privatization of schools, prisons and other government areas; labor law and voter ID legislation.

ALEC does not give money to candidates but it puts sitting republican legislators in the same room with corporations that have an interest in certain legislation. The legislators become advocates for the corporations. The Koch brothers for instance are major funders of ALEC and Koch Industries is a corporate member of ALEC's "Private Enterprise" Board and played a key role in boosting free trade agreements such as the Korea, Panama and Columbia agreements in Congress. Another ALEC Private Enterprise Board member was Coca Cola and its policies had been particularly effective in campaigning aggressively against soda taxes on sugary, unhealthy drinks, proposed by nutrition and health groups to state and federal legislators in order to lower obesity rates and raise much needed state revenue.

The national chairman of ALEC is Louisiana republican state representative Noble Ellington. In his interview with NPR, he described what ALEC stands for as the following: limited government, Jeffersonian principles, free trade and private sector growth to stimulate the economy. He stated that corporate members get a big say because they will be affected by the legislation. "I see corporations as friends and creators of jobs, adding to the wealth of individuals out there who are working for them, Ellington said. William Milton Cooper, author of *Behold A Pale Horse,* stated it most accurately, "It is paradoxical that the government body most representative of the American citizen is the one that has been the most easily subverted. Through PACs, payoffs, pork-barrel politics, professional politicians, congressmen who are members of secret societies and through greed and fear, our representatives and senators quit representing us long ago."

PRISON PRIVATIZATION

Corrections Corporation of America (CCA) is the largest private prison operation in the U.S. On its website it states that it currently partners with all three federal corrections agencies (the Federal Bureau of Prisons, The U.S. Marshalls Service, and Immigration and Customs Enforcement), nearly half of all states and more than a dozen local municipalities. Since its inception, CCA has maintained its market leadership position in private corrections, managing more than 50 percent of all beds under contract with such providers in the United States. The company joined the New York Stock Exchange in 1994 and now trades under the ticker symbol CXW. Forbes Magazine has named Corrections Corporation of America among "America's Best Big Companies".

Harley Lappin was the Director of the Federal Bureau of Prisons when I was incarcerated. I wrote letters to him during that time explaining the inequities of the federal prison system and encouraging him to instruct his agency to use existing ameliorative measures available to the Bureau to assist eligible incarcerated people to return to their families and communities. During his tenure Lappin had testified numerous times before Congress regarding overcrowding due to mandatory minimum sentencing for drugs. After twenty-five years at the agency Lappin retired after being arrested in February 2011 for drunk driving charges. Unlike most of the incarcerated people released from the Federal Bureau of Prisons, Lappin's court involvement did not preclude him from finding his next job. Corrections Corporation of America (CCA), the largest private prison manager and owner, hired him as Chief Corrections Officer. This hiring opened the door to CCA gaining access to the largest government operator of prisons in the country, Lappin's former employer, the Federal Bureau of Prisons.

In January 2012, on behalf of CCA, Harley Lappin presented the Corrections Investment Initiative to 48 states encouraging them to allow CCA to take care of all their incarceration needs. In exchange the participating prisons have to contain at least 1,000 beds that the states agree to keep mostly full, and the states must promise to pay CCA for operating the prisons for at least 20 years. The American Civil Liberties Union and a broad coalition of 60 policy and religious groups have urged states to reject CCA's offer.

United States taxpayers have expended over a trillion dollars building prisons and putting people in them. It is private prison companies such as Corrections Corporation of America that states are now looking to in order to balance their depleted budgets. Multiple reasons lead to the excess. One is the high cost of the Crime Control and Law Enforcement Act. Another is the numerous hard-on-crime laws that followed this enactment. Finally, cash strapped states across the country, in order to balance their budgets, proposed to sell their prisons to private companies. Then they contract with the new owners to operate them using taxpayer dollars. On the federal level, 18 percent of federal prisoners are now held within private facilities and according to the Huffington Post, nearly half of all immigrant detainees are now held in privately run detention facilities, even as the Feds continue to build new prisons.

Contrary to the private prison industry's claims of providing a stable employment base, the shift from government owned and operated prisons to the private sector is not supported by the effected employees. The Police Benevolent Association, which represents state corrections officers, said the privatization plan could put prison security at risk, with lower wages of private prisons forcing out veteran workers and increasing staff turnover and vacancies.[lxiii] The takeover of prisons by private entities usually results in pay cuts and loss of health care benefits. There is no question that the objective of these publicly traded, private prisons is to make money for their shareholders. It is not only that competitive pay and health benefits for employees are not maintained in these takeovers, neither is appropriate care and rehabilitation of those incarcerated. Turning over the government responsibility of corrections to private entities affects policy far beyond the area of criminal justice encroaching more and more upon labor law. For instance, there are more attempts to diminish collective bargaining rights and bust labor unions. The shares of private prison companies have climbed 11 percent annually in the past five years in the New York Stock Exchange. The circle widens. President Obama's budget request for fiscal year 2013 included cuts to everything from Medicare and Medicaid to defense and homeland security. Notwithstanding the President's budget proposal, the Federal Bureau of Prisons sought a forty-two percent increase, which would raise its budget to more than 6.9 billion dollars.

The Justice Department 2010 figures demonstrate 2.3 million adults in jail or prison in the U.S. This meant that 1 in 100 American adults were behind bars. This created a large pool of cheap, captive labor. One of the easiest places to get a job is in a prison as an incarcerated person. Huge segments of the free population in the U.S. who are not provided employment opportunities when on the streets, meaning not in prison, become completely employable once incarcerated. Jobs exist in abundance in prison. The only difference is the pay scale. Private companies are allowed to create jobs for incarcerated people and pay them little more than 12-25 cents per hour.

While many companies continue a holding pattern in hiring outside of prisons, notwithstanding a shocking build up of cash, there is a rapidly increasing number of companies taking advantage of the once surplus labor, now captive labor, within prisons. According to the Justice Policy Institute, the projected 2013 federal prison population is 229, 268 incarcerated people – 6,500 or more than 2012, an inevitable result of unfair drug laws, harsh sentencing laws and selective prosecution.

States such as Louisiana are allowed to contract out their jail population to work for private businesses. On average the incarcerated people are paid 50 cents per day. Many of the clean-up crews hired by BP for the Deepwater Horizon explosion in the Gulf of Mexico were incarcerated people who were paid a few cents an hour to clean up the toxic oil. There are many other companies that rely on prison labor for products sold in their stores such as K-Mart and J.C. Penny that both sell jeans made by incarcerated people in Tennessee prisons. In Wisconsin incarcerated people are paid wages ranging from twenty-two cents to $1.50 per hour to make products for Badger State Industries, the Wisconsin prison industries program, which raked in a $1.2 million annual profit.[lxiv]

The prison I was in was one of many federal prisons that participated in UNICOR, the federal prison industry, and there the women were paid up to $1.50 a day. The Correctional Industries Association predicted that by the year 2000, 30 percent of America's incarcerated population would have labored to create nearly $9 billion in sales for private business interests. Today, UNICOR alone generates over $500 million in sales annually and still pays its workers as little as 50 cents an hour.

Individuals released from prison, though employed while incarcerated, face the most difficult hurdle of reentering a job market already full of surplus labor. The majority of incarcerated people in both state and federal prisons are non-violent offenders who should have been eligible for community corrections and alternatives to incarceration. What they got was the harsh mandatory sentences that resulted in their incarceration. Had that eligible offender been allowed to remain in the community in lieu of incarceration, those with employment could have kept their jobs and those looking could still have been in a position to earn a sustainable income. Then they could have also contributed their sweat equity to the care of their families, pay taxes, as well as pay any restitution. They would have avoided the debilitating affects on employability and income eligibility that the stigma of incarceration carries. Incarceration not only has an economic effect on the community in which the offenders reside, it also has a permanent impact on their earning potential. The criminal justice system leaves economic scars on the incarcerated long after their formal involvement with the system has ended.[lxv]

Mass unemployment, mass incarceration, and mass disenfranchisement create an endless cycle of economic marginalization, stigmatization and social exclusion. Private prisons may be privately owned but are still supported by tax dollars. Not to mention, as stated so often by economist Manning Marable, they only continue to add an ever-widening circle of social disadvantage, poverty, and civil death, touching the lives of tens of millions of U.S. people.

CORPORATE CRIME

My first introduction to corporate anything was in the eighth grade. We learned about the stock market. We each had to select a company and follow its stock. I attended an elite private school in the East where many of the students came from some of the same families the campus buildings were named after, such as Greenleaf Hall. Capitalism was the 'C' in our ABCs. However, it wasn't until years later in college that I heard for the first time the term, "corporate welfare."

I was a college student taking my first economics class. Having always been afraid of anything related to numbers, I was sitting in class feeling inadequate. I was in a classroom full of white men and still, at that time in my life, feeling like I didn't belong there. I was the only woman and the only black person in the class, except for my hero, professor and economist, Jeremiah Cotton. Dr. Cotton loved black people and he was out to set the record straight in his classes. He introduced us to great scholars and activists like Manning Marable, and his book *How Capitalism Underdeveloped Black America,* and Jeffrey Reimer, *The Rich Get Richer and the Poor Get Prison*. Dr. Cotton showed us the true portrait of what groups make up the most welfare recipients in the United States. He taught us that the majority of people receiving welfare was white women and children and that the majority of black single mothers worked for a living. He introduced us to corporate welfare and explained that the percentage of tax dollars doled out for people welfare was miniscule in comparison to corporate welfare. Corporate welfare, he explained was in the form of subsidies costing taxpayers billions of dollars while driving corporate taxes down. Dr. Cotton taught us the true portrait between the two forms of welfare in this country, and Dr. Cotton taught us who received most of it. For me it was the beginning of learning to look beyond what the media and power brokers put forward as opposed to what is fact.

Why do we so readily attach labels, crack whore, dope fiend, junkie, labels that begin the dehumanization that creates the disconnect that allows us to so casually lock people in cages. To so casually take mothers from their children for ten years and longer for selling drugs. But what labels did we have for Goldman Sachs, Citigroup, Bank of America and the CEOs who commandeered the financial crisis that keeps our images of them in our collective minds as above incarceration. Nobody goes to jail is the mantra of the financial-crisis era, one that saw virtually every major bank and financial company on Wall Street embroiled in obscene criminal scandals that impoverished millions and collectively destroyed hundreds of billions, in fact, trillions of dollars of the world's wealth – and nobody went to jail.[lxvi]

The media and the general public define crime as acts committed by violent, psychopathic, mostly young, black males. Serious crimes occur daily at corporate headquarters in banks and on Wall Street. Prisoners tend to be poor yet in terms of economic loss, more crime is committed by the relatively affluent.[lxvii] Not a single bank or Wall Street CEO is in prison for defrauding millions of Americans. They robbed us and we're still paying for it in billions of dollars that far exceeds any dollar amount placed on street crime. Our perception of crimes committed by financial CEOs is different than the crimes of a drug addict running down the street with your television.

So we have to first develop critical thinking about what crime is and recognize that we have been conditioned about what we think is crime. You want to win elections, you bang on the jail-able class. You build prisons and fill them with people for selling dime bags and stealing CD players. But for stealing a billion dollars? For fraud that puts a million people into foreclosure? Pass. It's not a crime. Prison is too harsh.[lxviii] For example, in its 2001 report the FBI estimated that the nation's total loss from robbery, burglary, larceny-theft and motor vehicle theft in 2001 was $17.2 billion – less than a third of what Enron alone cost investors, pensioners and employees.[lxix] Long before our current financial shakedown on the American people by Wall Street and the banks, the total cost of white-collar crime in 1997 was $338 billion, more than 80 times the total amount stolen in all thefts reported by the FBI that year.[lxx]

Call me crazy, but what about the corporate crimes committed against the environment? The toxic chemicals in the waste generated by corporations have created such high levels of pollutants that it is now even affecting children in the womb. I read somewhere that a recent study detected chemicals in the blood of newborns from air-born pollutants. Corporate crimes against the environment are global. Years after being outlawed for manufacturing within the United States due to toxic levels, companies continue to release these toxins into the global environment by moving factories to countries with no environmental regulations.

The recent BP Deepwater Horizon spill and environmental disaster in the Gulf was such a devastating assault on the environment and on the respiratory systems of people living in the area, that even the clean up may be worse than the spill. Marine Toxicologist Susan Shaw explains that Corexit, the dispersant used to break up the oil, contains petroleum solvents and a chemical that ruptures red blood cells and causes internal bleeding in animals and people.

Corporations also cause more violence and death than street criminals. The U.S. national murder rate reported by the FBI is about 16,000 each year and violent crime has been steadily on the decline. However, these number do not include the thousands of annual deaths caused by cancer and other diseases linked to corporate pollution, defective products, tainted food, tobacco, and other causes. An estimated 553,400 people in the U.S. died from cancer in 2001.[lxxi]

It is interesting that when it comes to political finance laws corporations are people. However when it comes to holding corporations liable for the crimes they commit, somehow the corporate veil protects those same people. The crimes committed by the corporations are no less harmful, and often even more harmful on a global scale.

Understand my position here. I am not advocating for these CEOs to go to prison. Even for them I would advocate for harm reduction alternatives to incarceration. At least not as a front-line approach to correcting the harm caused. Maybe make the corporation financially accountable to a school system for example. CEOs can be egotistical and competitive. Make them pay for their greed through educating the most resource deprived communities and if the school under performs, then the CEO goes to prison.

We must change our misguided perception of what is a crime and how to deal with it. The same way we search for reasons not to put people on the elite corporate level in prison we must use that same discretion for non-violent offenders, particularly those suffering from the public health, not criminal, dilemma of addiction.

This is a real problem for me. I embarked on a mission for spiritual growth. I try and remain conscious about my thoughts without being sucked continuously down the vacuum packed tunnel of mind gibberish. I guard myself against whirlwind feelings of hatred. I've read countless self-help books, insight meditation guides and attended retreats to regroup my mind from acting like, as Buddhists say, a monkey. Everything I've read repeatedly reminds me of the importance of love. Love is divine. It lives within us. With love and good cheer flooding our spirits and infusing our hearts, the likes of confusion, doubt, worry, fear and unhappiness are no longer part of our daily experience.[lxxii] Still, I struggle daily with staying in loving kindness.

Sometimes I think that I am a little challenged. I have a tendency to take things very literally. Like when I convinced myself after reading the Secret that because my intentions were so good and focused on helping people, that using the money that belonged to my mortgage company clients, that eventually ended me up in federal prison, would somehow have a different outcome because I was following the Laws of Attraction to the letter. See what I mean. Most people would have enough sense not to admit such foolishness but my point in writing this is not to keep up the facade but really share my experiences truthfully that provided me with the need to speak up and have something to say. I now have something to say about the culture of prosecution.

That being said, I hate prosecutors. Obviously I am a work in progress. How does it get any better than that? Keeping it in the question is an energy tool my dear sisterfriend, Kass Thomas-Corbelli, taught me. She lives in a villa in Rome, married to the grandson of the man who built the villa, travels the world, speaks a million languages, practices some weird thing called Access Energy Consciousness (which apparently works). Her life is perfect…we hate her. She will read this and send me a clearing and encourage me to say something like "what would it take to love prosecutors… or, will I destroy and uncreate all that holds those feelings in place." I feel lighter already. So let me start over. I dislike the present culture of prosecution.

I wasn't going to write about prosecutorial misconduct even after collecting research on the subject for a long time because I didn't feel as though I could articulate my feelings without conveying the hatred that I do not want to continue to have. Prosecutorial misconduct was the one subject taking up most of the space in my storage bins I had crammed under my prison bunk. I mentioned this to my friends Tia and Monique one day in the TV room and they gasped at the thought of leaving out such an important part of a discussion about the need for sentencing reform and ending the war on drugs and mass incarceration. But every time I sat down to write about the subject of prosecutorial misconduct I just drew circles as if under a heaviness that moved over me as soon as I thought of the culture of prosecution. As a criminal defense attorney I worked for years with prosecutors. A prosecutor prosecuted me. I hate prosecutors. I know I need to get beyond this. It's not healthy and I don't hate any person, even those that choose to be prosecutors. Some years ago I attended a continuing legal education conference in Boston. It was a bi-partisan training on trial practice. Prosecutors were in attendance. An old school, highly experienced veteran defense attorney stood up and started his presentation with, "I come from a family of lawyers. My father was a lawyer, I am a lawyer, and my kids are lawyers. None of us have ever been a prosecutor. None of us will ever be a prosecutor. We just don't do prosecutor. We are defense attorneys. It's just who we are." That pretty much summed it up for me.

I worked in and around the criminal justice system for many years, even prior to becoming an attorney. Notwithstanding the steady parade of shackled Black men and women I worked to provide legal advocacy for within the criminal courts, I had no idea about the true impact of the federal and state sentencing guidelines and mandatory minimums in increasing the incarceration rate of Black and Hispanic poor people. Some in my profession would again be embarrassed to disclose this level of ignorance about something so critical to criminal defense work, however I know that most are not truly aware of the level of mass incarceration. It was not until being in the midst of it as a result of my own incarceration and actually witnessing life in a federal prison where women were being warehoused, that I became acutely aware of where that steady parade through the courthouses ended, and I was stunned and heart broken.

For years I had been aware of the protracted sentences on the federal level starting as far back as the mid eighties. In 1990 my husband, then boyfriend, Jon James, was sentenced to serve a 10-year federal sentence for his role in a drug conspiracy case out of Boston, Massachusetts. I was in college at the time and I remember writing letters to the editors of both the Boston Globe and the Herald newspapers about the unfairness in the length of the sentences for selling drugs. Due to my relationship with Jon, I knew many of the people who were part of this drug conspiracy. They were mostly very young Black men in their twenties from Queens, New York and Boston, Massachusetts, and Anywhere, Innercity, America. They had little education or skills training. Most wanted jobs but had been chronically unsuccessful at finding sustainable employment. During the late eighties and early nineties about twenty percent of young black men was neither in school nor working. Black average annual unemployment rates at that time had been over ten percent for more than twenty years.[lxxiii] Cocaine became excessively abundant throughout black urban communities and a too easy source of employment and income for the masses of unemployed young men. Prosecutors began an aggressive prosecution and incarceration push that included use of mandatory minimum sentences for crack possession or distribution. These mandatory sentences soon became plea bargain tools to get convictions.

It took more than 25 years for Congress to pass the Fair Sentencing Act, A first step in amending the discriminatory crack law that still incarcerates millions of predominantly poor black people to unreasonably long prison sentences for crack cocaine. Crack sentences had a 100:1 disparity between crack cocaine and the powder form of the same drug. In other words, with no scientific evidence to support a sentencing disparity, it took 100 times the amount of powder cocaine to get the same protracted sentence for crack cocaine. And even as Congress has recently amended the disparity they still didn't eliminate the sentencing difference completely. As of today there still remains a sentencing disparity of 18:1. To make matters more unjust, the amendment was not made retroactive to correct the unfairness in sentencing to those already incarcerated.

When the crack sentencing law was finally amended under the Fair Sentencing Act, federal prosecutors initially refused to back down, seeking to keep the 100:1 ratio in place for as long as possible. A Department of Justice memorandum dated August 5, 2010, regarding the Fair Sentencing Act of 2010, addressed to all U.S. Attorneys from H. Marshall Jarrett, Chief Counsel and Director of the United States Department of Justice. In it Director Jarrett instructed his nationwide team of federal prosecutors that "The new law will apply prospectively only to the offense conduct occurring on or after the date of the enactment. Accordingly, the previous threshold quantities (i.e., 5 grams for the five-year mandatory minimum and 50 grams for the ten-year mandatory minimum, will continue to apply for all offense conduct that occurred prior to the date of the enactment of the new law (i.e., August 3, 2010), regardless of whether the case was charged subsequent to enactment of the new law." In other words, the Fair Sentencing law was passed to correct the racist, classist, scientifically unsubstantiated disparity in crack sentences and even though Congress only partly corrected it by partially reducing the disparity to 18:1 and eliminating the five years for five grams mandatory minimum sentence, now the Department of Justice (prosecutors) was demanding judges to continue sentencing crack defendants to the old, unjust 100:1 crack to powder ratio, including the now eliminated 5 year mandatory minimum sentence, if the sale or possession of the drugs (offense conduct) pre-dated the August 3, 2010 enactment of the Fair Sentencing Act. Prosecutors do that kind of stuff.

The extraordinary complexity of the criminal justice system on both federal and state levels also make it impossible for a defendant to keep up. As retired California Judge J Richard Couzens points out, "California has an extraordinarily convoluted patchwork body of sentencing laws whose complexity serves as a trap for even the most experienced, diligent, and knowledgeable practitioner." Plea agreements that are not plea agreements in total but instead serve merely as the floor to which after a defendant signs an agreement, prosecutorial enhancements can be added to lengthen the sentence considerably. So a defendant for instance signs a plea agreement for a 10-year mandatory minimum and then at sentencing the prosecutor requests a 5-year enhancement over and above the underlying 10-year mandatory minimum. Prosecutors do that.

Another dangerous and ruthlessly wielded prosecutorial tool is the charge of conspiracy. Often the threat of the catchall charge of conspiracy is persuasive in a defendant's decision to forego a trial and accept a plea agreement. The charge of conspiracy is so vague and requires so little to prove, that apparently a person can even conspire with herself. It is the charge that if all else is weak in the case, the prosecution can go to conspiracy for a conviction. Whether alone or as an enhancement to other charges, it carries a serious sentencing wallop. Prosecutors do that.

And with all they have in their arsenal to convict and incarcerate, both state and federal prosecutors still, in study after study, demonstrate serious prosecutorial misconduct. An investigation by USA Today documented criminal cases in which Justice Department prosecutors repeatedly violated their duty to seek justice, not just convictions. Violating laws and ethics rules, federal prosecutors were found to be hiding evidence, lying to judges and juries, breaking plea agreements, and committing abuses so serious that innocent people have been put in prison. Prosecutors do this.

In 1963 the Supreme Court of the United States held in *Brady v. Maryland* that due process requires the prosecution to turn over evidence favorable to the accused and material to his guilt or punishment. In other words, prosecutors must disclose to defendants evidence that could help prove their innocence. It's a basic, fundamental rule of evidence that students are taught in law school. Discovery and trial preparation is not supposed to be a hide the ball experience. There's strategy involved in presenting your case but it's not about hiding evidence and cutting corners to win. Because prosecutors often campaign using tough-on-crime rhetoric, conditions often outweigh upholding the rights of the accused. The very nature of the act of withholding evidence is to intentionally and deceptively hide information. In a criminal justice system where most cases are resolved by plea agreements and evidence is not scrutinized the same way as when preparing for trial, withheld pieces to the puzzle could easily be overlooked. The USA Today study demonstrated cases so bad that judges threw out the cases. How many more people are in prison because intentionally withheld, exculpatory evidence was undisclosed by prosecutors and instead of taking the case to trial the defendant took a plea agreement. Prosecutors do that. There are numerous cases of prosecutorial intentional withholding of evidence that has led to people going to prison and even receiving the death penalty for crimes they did not commit, or exculpatory evidence should have been made available to them. But yet there is no crime for those intentional acts by prosecutors and most often they are excused from administrative sanctions because they are prosecutors.

Around the time of my case in Massachusetts Federal Court for the First District, there was also a case there where a United States Attorney was under investigation for prosecutorial misconduct for her egregious error in failing to produce plainly important exculpatory information to a defendant.[lxxiv] This error extended "a dismal history of intentional and inadvertent violations of the government's duties to disclose in cases assigned to this court". [lxxv] The defendant was charged with being a felon in possession of a firearm. If convicted of that charge, he would have been subject to a mandatory ten-year sentence.

As described by United States District Judge in his decision, the defendant filed a motion to suppress, alleging that the police did not have the reasonable suspicion necessary to justify the seizure and the search of him that led to the discovery of the firearm at issue. As the court has previously explained:

[I]n an effort to justify the seizure of the defendant, the government argued, and the Boston Police Officer falsely testified, that there was justification to stop the defendant because, despite the dark and the distance between them, he identified the defendant as he rode his bicycle down a street in Dorchester, Massachusetts. The officer testified that his suspicions were raised when the defendant pedaled away from him because the officer knew him and he had never avoided him before. However, the officer had on several earlier occasions told the lead prosecutor in this case that he did not recognize the defendant on the Dorchester street and did not identify the man who had been on the bicycle as the defendant until later, when other officers had tackled him at another location. The officer's important inconsistent statements were not disclosed to the defendant until the court conducted an in camera review of the U.S. attorney's notes, just before the suppression hearing was complete. The U.S. attorney and her supervisor acknowledged that the officer's prior inconsistent statements constituted material exculpatory evidence, and that the failure to disclose them violated the government's constitutional duty under *Brady* v. *Maryland*, 373 U.S. 83 (1963), its progeny, and the court's orders. Ultimately, the court decided not to sanction the United States attorney, having provided her an opportunity to demonstrate that she would not withhold evidence again and "the U.S. attorney has continued her exceptional efforts to assure that her error is not repeated."[lxxvi]

In my own case, I was sentenced to federal prison for 24 months for pleading guilty to mail and wire fraud. The fact that I was an attorney was also used against me by the prosecution in requesting a two-level upward sentencing adjustment for me under section 3B1.3 of the United States Sentencing Guidelines for "abusing a position of trust in my capacities as an attorney." I wanted to ask for the same consideration for myself in my situation as the U.S. attorney asked of the Court after she knowingly withheld evidence in the hopes of continuing to use illegally and unconstitutionally acquired evidence in order to get a conviction against the defendant. I was counseled not to raise this issue, as it would only take away from my demonstrating to the court my acceptance of responsibility for my base offense. In my capacity as a real estate conveyance attorney I represented banks and mortgage companies and I misappropriated 1.2 million dollars in loan proceeds. I did it. Although completely misguided, my intention was always to help homeowners in my community who were in imminent danger of losing their homes to foreclosure. Of course, my actions spiraled into a hodgepodge of complicated juggling to unravel good intentions gone awry due to my willingness to side step ethical and fiduciary responsibilities I had sworn to uphold. I accepted full responsibility for my actions and self-reported my offense to the authorities. The consequences were grave and are ongoing. I was incarcerated in a federal prison. I am re-paying 1.2 million dollars in restitution to predatory lenders who received a bail out for their predatory offenses never deemed criminal, and the U.S. Attorney's office (the prosecutors) encouraged the IRS to also apply a discretionary tax fine against me for my misconduct "in my role as an attorney in a position of trust", adding an additional $500,000 to my overall sentence, essentially giving me a lifetime of protracted punishment.

My view of hoping to not receive the enhanced punishment because I was an attorney at the time of my misconduct was, in my opinion, against the predatory lenders that came into my community and lured homeowners into criminal and nefarious make-believe mortgage products that eventually financially devastated working families. Lenders that came into poor and working communities and conned and fast-talked homeowners into borrowing more money than they could afford and more money than their homes were worth. The lenders allowed appraisers to artificially raise property values while the title insurance companies made millions of dollars on mortgage title insurance policies, turning a blind eye to the predatory lending frenzy. It was referred to as predatory lending because of the predatory types of mortgage products that were whimsically thought up by greedy Wall Street financiers. Products like no doc loans, interest only loans, adjustable rate mortgages, and the use of first and second mortgages.

I did not want to have my actions trickle down to any homeowner that got inadvertently tangled up in my mess. I self-reported my offense to the authorities in order to keep this from happening. I expected the prosecutors to help in mitigating any harm to the borrowers by reporting and confirming to the lenders that those mortgages had not been paid off due to my malfeasance and not due to any inaction by the borrowers. The prosecutors did nothing to inform the lenders of this throughout the entire almost two-year period it took them to prosecute me. At my sentencing hearing, in addition to being accused of getting pregnant to avoid prison, the prosecutor suggested that I should be more severely punished because I continued my work with at-risk girls through my long-standing education project, Career Roadmap for Girls, and in the words of the prosecutor, "held myself out as a role model even after being prosecuted". Also, the fact that my actions had trickled down to affect borrowers after the U.S attorney's office did nothing to mitigate the damage, was raised by the prosecutor in an effort to justify his request to put me in prison for five years. It still doesn't sit right with me that there was an opportunity to avoid harm to the borrowers but because I had committed the offense of misappropriating the money, nothing was going to be done to mitigate the harm, and then the more serious result was going to be used against me at sentencing. So yes. I was pissed off because things don't happen in a vacuum. My crime was against mean, nefarious, greedy mortgage lenders, not borrowers. Not families in my community that I had committed my entire professional and personal life to help empower and advocated on behalf of. And I too, like the U.S. attorney that withheld exculpatory evidence, deeply regretted my actions done as an attorney, and hoped for the same consideration provided her when I asked the Court to not give me the sentencing enhancement requested by the prosecutor. I was found to have violated my position of trust, as asked for by the U.S. Attorney. Thankfully I was not sentenced to the 63 months as requested by the prosecutors. Judge Woodlock of the 1st Circuit sentenced me to 24 months, a wide departure from the guidelines. For his consideration of my entire self, personally and professionally, I am profoundly grateful. I was very fortunate to have received this lesser sentence.

Over-zealous prosecutorial practices have led to a culture of misconduct within prosecution offices throughout the country. There are numerous examples of this, The Central Park Five being in my lifetime one of the most egregious recent events. Prosecutors who withhold exculpatory evidence are clearly abusing a position of trust in their capacity as an attorney and their position as a prosecutor should not be a veil of protection for their accountability. And so too do I need to continue working on my own evolution.

Danbury Federal Prison has had its share of famous and politically connected people pass through its doors. Leona Helmsley, the Watergate guys, Reverend Sung Young Moon. While I was there our state senator from Massachusetts, Diane Wilkerson, was sentenced to 3.5 years for "attempted extortion" for taking $23,000 in alleged bribe money. Around the same time Senator arrived, came the wife of a Massachusetts congressman, who despite prosecutor's request for a sentence of only probation, served a 30-day sentence for aiding and abetting the filing of false tax returns. In a shocking turn-around from its customary aggressive style of prosecution and requests for upward departures of the sentencing guidelines for most defendants, the prosecutor requested that she receive 90 days on house arrest plus two years probation. He noted that she was a first-time offender, the wife of a congressman, and her conviction had drawn media attention and shame that served as its own punishment.[lxxvii]

Prison Legal News is a publication that I personally believe to be one of the most important pieces of media published in this country. It is a monthly magazine and on-line periodical that provides review and analysis of prisoners' rights, court rulings and news. In the past it has published articles about some of the rare cases in which people with political connections who commit crimes have received prison sentences comparable to those routinely given to defendants without such connections. In one such article it reported that the congressman's wife's case was "one of three in as many weeks in which federal courts rejected special treatment for people with political connections. The two other cases the article referred to were the above-mentioned case of Massachusetts' senator, Diane Wilkerson and Boston city councilor Chuck Turner, who at 70 years old was implicated for taking an alleged $1,000 bribe and sentenced to 3 years in federal prison.

What Prison Legal News failed to report was that prior to the above-mentioned cases, two former consecutive Massachusetts House Speakers had been convicted of federal crimes but evaded prison sentences, and were "welcomed back like they were some sort of heroes" at state house ceremonies. They were powerful white men who had been in political leadership roles in Massachusetts for years and like so many others before them, had evaded prison. Had it not been for the incarceration of the female Black senator, Diane Wilkerson and Black city counselor, Chuck Turner, even the most recent former Massachusetts House Speaker to be convicted of seven counts in his public corruption case, including two counts of mail fraud, three counts of wire fraud and extortion, I believe, would be a free man today. And again, I am not advocating for his or the other MA speakers of the House incarceration. It's not the answer.

Here's where Prison legal news got it wrong. Wilkerson and Turner, both black politicians were overly-sentenced to federal prison for political crimes. The above-mentioned white former Massachusetts Speakers of the House received no prison time. Even when sentencing the congressman's wife to just 30-days, U.S. District Court Judge William G. Young stated, "She should get the sentence that anyone else would get." She didn't. Much to the pissed-off, similarly charged, women at Danbury who were also "first-time offenders" whose cases had drawn media attention and shame that they felt served its own punishment. They on the other hand were serving years, not thirty days.

When she arrived at Danbury she was a target for scorn and resentment by the women. Some of them posted news clippings of her 30-day sentence on the bulletin boards in an uncommon act of exposing her crime and special treatment.

In response to one of these articles and in an effort to use the media attention to raise awareness of the plight of the women, I wrote the following letter to the editors of a few newspapers:

Dear Editor,

I am incarcerated in the federal prison for women in Danbury, Connecticut. Your paper has recently reported on the sentencing of the wife of a Massachusetts congressman to this same place. The women here are angry about rumors that the newest admit was sentenced to only 30 days. They are angry about the special treatment they feel she has received as a wife of a congressman. I've encouraged them to look on the bright side of things.

Maybe during her thirty-day stay she will notice the plight of the women she will be visiting. Maybe she will be sleeping next to and sharing meals with the other first-time, non-violent offenders who also made a mistake but are serving 120 months under harsh federal mandatory minimum and guideline sentences. The same sentences her attorney, Donald Stern, advocated for and used to prosecute so many poor, black, first-time offenders during his reign as U.S. Attorney under the Clinton Administration.

Maybe while reaching into her prison locker some morning to make a cup of coffee she will glance over and see into another first-time offender's locker and see the pictorial history of that woman's children and how they've grown over the years into adulthood while their mother was warehoused in Danbury. Maybe she will become aware of how sentencing that mother to such a harsh and long sentence has been a waste of taxpayer money and even more tragic, a waste of human potential. Maybe she will discover that there are currently more than 2 million children in this country with one or both parents incarcerated and that she is sitting next to many such mothers, grandmothers, sisters, and daughters who manage to hold it together while dealing with a torrent of regret, heartache, remorse, alienation, loneliness and a host of other problems related to being warehoused in a prison while too often their children suffer and struggle to survive.

And maybe she will leave after her 30-day stay and become a voice on the outside for the real faces of the women in the federal prison system and she will be inspired to speak about and advocate for sentencing reform and give those women she left behind the second chance that she received at the outset.

Having grown up in Roxbury, Massachusetts, within both of the political districts of Senator Diane Wilkerson and City Councilor Chuck Turner, it was difficult for me to accept their sentences particularly because sitting in a federal prison I knew first-hand the colossal waste of sending either of them to one. Senator had been in office for 16 years and although City Councilor Turner had held his official political seat for only a few years, he had been at the forefront of every people movement and political progress from the grassroots on up, for as long as I can remember. They both gave a voice to a community that consistently did not have a voice or seat at the table and does not now have in their absence. While we were together in Danbury Senator would often share letters from folks in the community thanking her for the many things she accomplished for our community that continue to grow and have a positive impact.

I still support Prison Legal News and it is among my top reading choices. I still encourage people to subscribe to it as a necessary addition to everyone's sources of information. But I am sorry that I did not send my thoughts to them about how I respectfully believe they misaligned news stories by lumping Senator Diane Wilkerson and City Councilor Chuck Turner into a story that truly should have been not been about them having not received special treatment, but about a reversal of roles where race played a role in creating a backlash that forced an end to the special treatment of white politicians who commit crimes in Massachusetts.

TEN DAYS AND A WAKE UP

For me, the thing about prison is that I was always scared that I might never get out of there. I was afraid that I was going to fall through the cracks and get lost in the system. There was always that evil feeling in the air that they would lose you. To add to this fear, the prison staff had the discretion to determine your out date, whether sooner than later, or more halfway house time or less. They withheld this information for as long as possible so a person never had a clear understanding of when they were going to be released. Not to mention that the feds require incarcerated people to serve 85 percent of their sentence and there is no federal parole as it was eliminated with the enactment of the federal sentencing guidelines in 1984.

We were always counting and re-counting the days until we could go home. Every day we counted. How many days left to the week, month, season, year. How many months to my next evaluation. How much time before the next count. How many hours before we can turn out these damn florescent lights hanging directly over our bunks. And when it finally gets close to your release date, you start counting down how many days and a wake up. I did know two things for sure. First, It was absolutely a waste of taxpayer money to put me in a prison and let me sit there with absolutely nothing to do except for a job making twelve cents an hour working in a damp, cold, prison garage, when I had a million dollar restitution I had to pay for a crime I committed against private, for-profit, greedy, predatory lenders. Two, I knew I had to try and land a different prison job other than standing in that wet, cold garage changing the oil of prison vehicles that for all I cared the engines could fall out of. I had to get into the education department and get a job teaching GED classes or else I knew for sure that I would sink even deeper into the same depression that helped land me in there.

I finally got a job teaching English, science and English-as-a-second language and switched my focus to transitioning sooner than later from the prison to a halfway house in Boston closer to my husband and children. After all, there is a federal law, Title 18, section 3621(b), part of the Second Chance Act, that establishes the criteria for an incarcerated person's eligibility for up to a year halfway house placement, and I met all of the requirements. I just knew I was on my way out of Danbury to a placement in Boston and I started preparing my written request to the prison administrator.

At the same time out in the world there was constant media attention on a new focus on proposed measures to reduce the cost of incarceration on the state and federal levels due to budget necessities. The mainstream attention to the issue was new but voices of reform advocates and families of the incarcerated for years had been calling out for both front-end sentencing alternatives as well as reentry initiatives that are both rehabilitative and would save millions of taxpayer dollars currently spent on warehousing people in prisons.

The 2011 budget appropriated to the Federal Bureau of Prisons was 6.7 billion dollars for the cost of housing over 200,000 federal incarcerated people, the majority non-violent offenders. Because prisons serve a purpose of holding those who have been ordered removed from society as punishment for breaking laws that vary from tax evasion to murder, there is a need for varied security level facilities to carry out that mandate. As a result, the Federal Bureau of Prisons has been granted wide latitude, wielding practically unchecked decision-making power under the guise of "discretion", in how they fulfill its mandate to incarcerate. This "discretion" allows the Bureau of Prisons to ignore even the laws enacted by Congress, as demonstrated through a systemic pattern of reinterpreting statutes that allow for reentry for eligible people, regardless of the intent of Congress to provide a pathway to more productive, cost-effective community-based alternatives to being idle in a prison at a huge cost to taxpayers.

The Second Chance Act, as it is referred to, authorizes the Federal Bureau of Prisons to grant to incarcerated people who participate in reentry preparation up to twelve months placement in a halfway house. Full implementation of this could provide huge savings. Halfway houses are less expensive and maximize the time of rehabilitative programming in the person's home community. Armed with the reading of the Act and related case law, I wrote my judge considering he had mentioned that there was no benefit to my incarceration except to avoid a sentencing disparity under the U.S. sentencing guidelines. I asked for his recommendation that I be placed in the Boston area halfway house. I also put my request in writing to the prison administration asking for a year of halfway house placement.

During the sentencing process, nobody talks about transitioning a person out of prison. The discussion of reentry of the person after incarceration is not typically covered, notwithstanding the absolute importance in whether your judge referenced your reentry and halfway house time during sentencing to provide guidance to the Bureau of Prisons as to when to release you from prison custody. I soon discovered that applying for reentry, even when following step-by-step the enumerated statutes created to reenter eligible people, sooner than later, doing so was more like falling down a rabbit hole of discretionary twists and turns and by the time you get it or are denied it, you've served most of your sentence in a prison anyway.

The prison administration completely ignored my first request. The U.S. Attorney's office that prosecuted me did not however. They responded to my letter-motion to my judge, albeit eight months later, with a "Government's Opposition to Defendant's Motion to Amend Judgment." In it they responded by stating "Defendant Andrea Goode-James has filed a *pro se* motion to amend her sentence which was imposed in December 2009. Because there is no legal basis for granting the relief requested, the motion should be denied." The government's response goes on to state that the Court sentenced Goode-James on December 7, 2009 to twenty-four months in the custody of the Bureau of Prisons, with a recommendation that she be designated to FCI Danbury or another institution closest to her relatives. I forgot to mention earlier that the reentry statute Title 18, section 3621(b) and its case law make it clear that a halfway house serves as another form of incarceration and a "prisoner placed in a halfway house is still under the control of the Federal Bureau of Prisons". So even though Congress had enacted and President Obama had signed into law the Second Chance Act that encouraged reentry of eligible incarcerated people into their communities, and my judge had recommended I be designated to Danbury, "*or another institution closest to her relatives*", the prosecutor claimed there was no legal basis for the judge to make a recommendation after sentencing that I be placed in the Boston halfway house. The Government cited federal statute, 18. U.S.C. Section 3582, which limits a Court's authority to modify or correct a sentence of imprisonment, which in practice makes null and void the new statute enacted to encourage reentry. It is absolutely dizzying and demonstrates a huge disconnect between legislative, judicial and executive branches of our government in terms of making productive change in the much needed area of sentencing reform. Title 18 U.S.C Section 3582 along with the "discretion" afforded the Federal Bureau of Prisons, renders the Second Chance Act regarding reentry practically useless. A toothless piece of legislation.

In September 2010, the prison administration denied my latest request to be transferred to the Boston halfway house.

The denial stated "*Review of your case reveals you require extremely limited transition assistance. For this reason, the Unit Team will refer you for Home Detention beginning on your Home Detention Eligibility Date (7/24/2011). If you feel you have release needs that are not addressed please communicate that need to the Unit team in writing at your next scheduled Team meeting.*" By the way, your children are not a transition need according to the Federal Bureau of Prisons. So there you have it. Although I met all of the eligibility criteria under Title 18, Section 3621 for placement in a halfway house for up to 12 months, those same positives designated me as "*requiring extremely limited transition assistance*" and therefore from the discretion of the Federal Bureau of Prisons, I had to remain in a prison in Danbury, Connecticut until a home confinement eligibility date almost a year later. The prison administrator summed it up best when I raised the issue with him of cost-effectiveness of halfway houses over prison beds. His response was "What is cost-effective for us about sending you to a halfway house?"

The Federal Bureau of Prisons is an agency with a mandate to incarcerate and has a budget reliant upon the incarceration of people. By not handling well the transition of statutorily eligible people into their communities the Bureau underutilizes alternatives while continuing to request annual budget increases from Congress. Now that over 2.5 million adult Americans are behind bars, failure to implement existing ameliorative statutes, as well as the practice of reinterpreting statutes, such as the Second Chance Act, while continuing a pattern of money chasing to fund prisons due to over-incarceration, fully exemplifies the Federal Bureau of Prison's unchecked waste of taxpayer money and the human potential of people eligible of reentering their communities and rejoining their families. U.S. Supreme Court Justice Anthony Kennedy stated "A people confident in its laws and institutions should not be ashamed of mercy…A decent and free society, founded in respect for the individual, ought not run a system with a sign at the entrance for incarcerated people saying, 'Abandon Hope, All Ye Who Enter Here.'"

AFTERWORD

What can you do to help reform the criminal justice inequities discussed in this book? You can join us at Families for Justice as Healing. We are a criminal Justice reform organization. Our primary focus is women and the impact of incarceration on their children.

Here's how you can get involved:

- Make a donation to support our ongoing work.
- Purchase at least one of our handmade dishcloths on a monthly basis, and ask friends to do the same. Our dishcloth campaign helps pay our operating expenses.
- Support our FREE HER campaign.
- Support our efforts to reform drug sentencing laws and reinstate federal parole.
- Further educate yourself on why drug use is a public health vs. criminal justice issue and why we must legalize and regulate all drugs in order to reform the criminal justice system.
- Use your voice. Talk about these issues with your neighbors and form a criminal justice reform working group in your community. We can help.

Information is available at
www.justiceashealing.org

BIBLIOGRAPHY

i *Emotional Intelligence,* Daniel Goleman
ii Manny Marable
iii *Power, Politics and Crime,* William J. Chambliss
iv *Golden Gulag,* Ruth Wilson Gilmore
v Paglen with Ruth Wilson Gilmore
vi Luna & Cassell
vii *Id*
viii *Id*
ix *Power, Politics and Crime,* William J. Chambliss
x *The Soul of the Law*, Benjamin Sells
xi *The Spiritualization of the Legal Profession,* David Hall, p. 62
xii Id at p. 109
xiii Id at 117
xiv Calafat et al, 2005
xv Maffini 2006
xvi The Boston Globe
xvii Prison Policy Initiative
xviii Rebecca Project for Human Rights
xix *Texas Tough,* Robert Perkinson
xx Malika Saada Saar
xxi Dr. Kathleen Hawk-Sawyer
xxii Garcia Coll, Surrey, Buccio-Notaro & Molla
xxiii New York Daily News
xxiv Barbara Bloom
xxv U.S. GAO
xxvi Impact of Parental Arrest and Incarceration
xxvii Id
xxviii The Vera Institute of Justice
xxix *Texas Tough,* Robert Perkinson

xxx Vera Institute of Justice
xxxi Gabel
xxxii Denise Johnson
xxxiii Fleet Maul
xxxiv Manning Marable
xxxv Fleet Maul
xxxvi *The Raft Is Not the Shore,* Thich Nhat Hahn, Daniel Berrigan
xxxvii *Buddha's Brain,* Dr. Rick Hanson
xxxviii Journal of the House - Massachusetts
xxxix The Sentencing Project
xl *Id*
xli Bureau of Justice Statistics
xlii Othello Harris, P. Robin Miller
xliii *Id*
xliv *Perpetual Prisoner Machine,* Joel Dyer
xlv Brennan Center for Justice
xlvi ACLU-Maryland
xlvii Urbanhabitat.org
xlviii New York Times
xlix USA Today
l *The Perpetual Prisoner Machine,* Joel Dyer
li Fleet Maul
lii Graber
liii The *Perpetual Prisoner Machine,* Joel Dyer
liv *Id*
lv *The Alchemy of Nine Dimensions,* Barbara Hand Clow
lvi *Id*
lvii Stephen Kiesling
lviii *Id*
lix Black's Law Dictionary, ninth edition
lx Steven Brill

lxi New York Times

How to Take on the Gun Industry, Ali Winston and Darwin Bond Graham, Truthout/ Interview

lxiii Federal USA

lxiv Overback

lxv Crutchfield and Pitchford

lxvi Matt Taibbi

lxvii *The Politics of Punishment,* Erik Olin Wright

lxviii Matt Taibbi

lxix Center for Corporate Policy

lxx *The Rich Get Richer, The Poor Get Prison,* Jeffrey Reimer

lxxi Center for Corporate Policy

lxxii *Secrets of the Light,* Dannion Brinkley

lxxiii Bureau of Labor Statistics

lxxiv *United States* v. *Jones*, 609 F. Supp 2d (d. Mass. 2009)

lxxv *Id*

lxxvi *Id*

lxxvii Reuters

Made in the USA
San Bernardino, CA
02 October 2018